P9-ELQ-629

Eat Tea

Traditional Chinese brick of tea.

Eat Tea

A New Approach to Flavoring Contemporary and Traditional Dishes

Joanna Pruess

with John Harney

The Lyons Press

Guilford, Connecticut

An imprint of The Globe Pequot Press

The Lyons Press is an imprint of The Globe Pequot Press.

Printed in the United States of America

10 9 8 7 6 5 4 3 2 1

Design by A Good Thing, Inc.

The Library of Congress Cataloging-in-Publication Data is available on file.

ISBN 1-58574-350-X

Contents

Foreword

Tea drinking is an ancient human invention, and tea is—next to water—the most widely consumed beverage on the planet. I have hopes that in this country, the public will discover tea in a very big way. Already, a smattering of tea shops and tea bars is opening across America. Americans are discovering the wide variety of teas distributed by large importers of fine tea. Green tea, which has been widely consumed in Asian countries for centuries, has now inspired new consumers around the world. The Tea Association of the United States reported that in the last decade sales of the drink grew from $1.8 billion to $4.6 billion. Green tea has been found to have anticancer effects, strong antioxidant

activity, and antibacterial effects and to boost both immune and detoxification functions. It has thus become viewed by both consumers and medical scientists as a "functional food," delivering a multitude of health benefits as well as great refreshment.

Green tea currently is the most popular beverage in Japan. It is not uncommon for people there to consume five or more cups of green tea daily. While canned and bottled green tea is now widely available in supermarkets and vending machines, these tend not to be of high quality. Yet the availability of green tea is allowing health-conscious individuals to consume a liter or more of green tea daily.

Unlike black tea, green tea is made by steaming fresh tea leaves at high temperatures; this inactivates the enzymes which break down the beneficial polyphenol component. The polyphenols are thus found at significantly higher levels in green tea than in black tea. The major polyphenol found in green tea, ECGC, is twenty times more powerful an antioxidant than vitamin E and two hundred times more powerful than vitamin C. These polyphenols also have anti-inflammatory effects. Numerous studies have suggested that green tea has the potential to reduce esophageal cancer, skin cancer, coronary heart disease, and many bacterial infections, including tooth decay and influenza.

 I believe that it is no coincidence that Asian men living in Asian countries have one thirtieth the incidence of fatal prostate cancer as American men; or that Japanese women living in Japan have one seventh the incidence of fatal breast cancer as American women. Numerous studies suggest that phytonutrients, like green tea, soy, omega-3 fatty acids, and seaweed, play a role. In a 1998 study, Harvard University scientists found that drinking one cup of tea daily lowered the risk of heart attack by up to 44 percent for tea drinkers compared with non-tea drinkers. Meanwhile, we continue to see strong hints in human-population studies that tea is beneficial. A 1995 study of cancer in postmenopausal women in Iowa revealed an inverse association between tea consumption (presumably, this would have been mostly black tea) and cancer risk for esophageal, stomach, and kidney cancers. In other words, drinking tea reduced the chance of developing these cancers.

An intriguing report came from Itaro Oguni, PhD, at the University of Shizuoka in Japan in 1989. He compiled statistics showing that the mortality rate from total cancers and also from stomach cancer (one of the predominant Japanese malignancies) were significantly lower in Shizuoka Prefecture, the leading tea-producing area in Japan.

Finally, I believe I have saved the best for last. If the evidence of Japanese researchers is to be believed, it may well be that the growth rates of already- developed cancers are radically slowed when green tea is consumed in sufficient quantities. Doctors at the Saitama Cancer Center in Japan made a study of the survival rates of patients with cancer relative to their green tea consumption. The astonishing results showed that patients who drank more than ten cups per day died 4.5 years (men) to 6.5 years (women) later than did patients who drank fewer than three cups per day. Relatively few conventional cancer treatments claim comparable statistical impact.

Green tea, the phytonutrient champ, has also been shown to lower cholesterol levels and reduce the rate of stroke, perhaps because of another phytonutrient found in tea, known as catechins. Platelets are the little saucer-shaped cells necessary to blood clotting. However, if they clump together excessively, they can block up an artery, causing a heart attack or stroke. Catechins make the platelets in the bloodstream less sticky thus reducing the risk that they'll clump.

Tea polyphenols have also been found to be strong inhibitors of the acquired immunodeficiency syndrome (AIDS) virus replication system. In addition, they possess antibacterial and antifungal properties. In experimental studies, for example, tea polyphenols have been found to enhance B-cells, a key part of our immune system. In Japan, a study was done in which tea was given to the students at one school, who gargled with it in an attempt to counteract an influenza outbreak that was then raging. The researchers concluded that it was quite effective and noted that no class in the school was closed during the outbreak.

The Harneys and Joanna Pruess have compiled the most remarkable recipes using green teas that I have ever seen. Cooking with green tea can allow us to focus and concentrate the dozens of phytonutrients found in this beverage into our diet. The nice thing about these recipes is that they make it very simple and easy to take in the nutritional benefits of green tea throughout each day. This book provides a wonderful and exciting road map to discovering and using the healing powers of green tea.

—Mitchell L. Gaynor, M.D.
Medical Director,
Director of Medical Oncology
Joan and Sanford I. Weill Medical College
Center for Complementary and Integrative Medicine

A Word from John Harney

It's not that I'm a stranger to cooking with tea; it's just because I'm slow about getting around to things that obviously need doing (ask my wife) that I am beginning to write this introduction to the subject of cooking with tea a mere thirty years after entering the tea business. Making tea my business was a sort of logical outcome to my lifelong connection with tea. I'm Irish and Ireland has been leading per capita European tea consumption for going on two centuries. My love of tea may be genetic.

Cornell University, in the days when I was getting my undergraduate degree in the School of Hotel Management, did a perfunctory job at best of exposing us to tea education. Not even I needed to be told that any leading hotel was expected to lay on a semi-formal afternoon tea that called for a marriage with special foods and specific flavors. However, most of us were left to our own devices when it came to brewing and serving tea. Cooking with tea was, for the most part, unheard of, much less taught.

Nonetheless, I must admit I've cooked with tea all my life both personally and professionally. This doesn't mean I want credit for original thinking: Nothing could be more ancient than cooking with tea. It's just that I've always enjoyed experimenting with whatever I found in the kitchen, and ownership of an inn in a Connecticut village helped. It allowed me to settle down and raise my family as well as spend a lot of time in the kitchen with a tea kettle as constant companion.

Our hostelry, the White Hart Inn located on the village green of Salisbury, Connecticut, served a pretty fair afternoon tea but we seldom had many takers except for the weekends when the neighboring Hotchkiss School parents swarmed in to attend games. Nevertheless, teatime around the fireplace in the inn's reception parlor is still a picture postcard of New England I retain and cherish; it's both rural and sophisticated in exactly the right degree, like tea itself.

My education continued when a Chinese chef I respected persuaded me to become his partner in a Chinese restaurant. I have no doubt that no other Connecticut Yankee in those distant days ever learned more about Chinese cooking or tea than I did from Danny Yushan Lee, my friend for life who is now an Associate Professor of culinary arts at the Culinary Institute of America.

When we met—to show you how things change—neither I nor anybody I knew had ever tasted green tea. Danny fixed that in a hurry and showed me how he used it to poach fish, too. His tea lore was good preparation, it turned out, for meeting Stanley Mason, Esquire.

Mr. Mason was not a New Englander. He originally came from Salisbury, in England, and had retired to our village out of nostalgia for the name itself. By the time we became friends he and Mrs. Mason were already elderly. Stanley had apprenticed in the tea trade in London back in its heyday before World War One. Old men in the firm he worked for remembered the great clipper ship races to beat the fleet to London from China with the first tea of the new season. He'd retired after a lifetime in the tea trade in New York but couldn't get tea out of his blood. Having established the Sarum Tea Company—Sarum was the Roman name for Salisbury in England—he happily continued to buy and sell tea, although in minuscule quantities.

With his connections and his knowledge, Stanley could take justifiable pride that his Sarum Tea was unsurpassed anywhere in the United States at that time. It wasn't long before the White Hart served nothing else and our customers began to ask where they could buy it for home use. Before much longer, the inn's county store became the leading outlet for Sarum Tea, if not the only one. And therein lay the rub.

As Stanley's years multiplied, so did my demands upon him to supply us with ever increasing amounts of tea. Mrs. Mason would reproach me and Mr. Mason would sometimes be apologetic: The only jasmine available wasn't good enough to blend with his Choicest Formosa Oolong to create his cherished Countess of Salisbury blend. "Just let me show you," he'd say, and soon I was receiving another impromptu lesson in another of the mysteries of tea.

Quality was Mr. Mason's primary concern, and I feel he taught me how to produce a tea of quality. It took me years to talk Stanley into selling a Hot Cinnamon spiced tea. (He thought I was prostituting the damned stuff.)

It seemed only natural, therefore—and to Mrs. Mason a vast relief—when Stanley eventually decided the only way to carry on was to sell his little tea company to me, his part-time apprentice and biggest customer. "Don't worry," he assured me. "I'll introduce you to my famous importer friend, Bill MacMelville, to take my place." Along with his knowledge, I inherited all of Mr. Mason's extensive contacts in the quality end of the trade.

There was no replacing Stanley, but in 1970, in partnership with my co-owners of the Inn, I did buy Sarum and meet Bill MacMelville. The first thing I discovered was what I needed most was a customer to replace the White Hart Inn, which after 23 years my partners and I finally sold. As part of my share I kept Sarum and resolved to have only family members as partners from then on. And then Stanley died in 1980, leaving me in the tea business on my own.

It was all I could do to sell six thousand pounds of tea in my first twelve months of ownership. My wife took a long look at my sales figures and began studying for a realtor's license. Then one day I received a phone call from a man in San Francisco who introduced himself as James Norwood Pratt and said he was writing a book about tea. Judging from his manner on the phone, he seemed to be getting along in years, but I thought I recalled a book on wine by a writer of that name and hoped he'd do as well by the "cups that cheer but do not inebriate." I enjoyed our conversation and some months later was overjoyed to see it quoted in his book *The Tea Lover's Treasury*.

A little recognition provides a lot of encouragement. Here was a statement of credibility from a recognized tea authority that I could put to good use. The trickle of mail order business it engendered showed me the value of publicity, too. A company like ours was just what lovers of quality tea all over the country were on the lookout for. But were they numerous enough to allow me to support my family?

It was with no small amount of anxiety and uncertainty that I dropped the name Sarum in the spring of 1983 and Harney & Sons Fine Teas was born. I think I added the "& Sons" partly out of loneliness at the time. It was clearly wishful thinking, for I was in no position to hire even one of my four sons nor could I be sure they'd share my growing love for tea. But I thought I saw the way forward.

With my background in the hotel business, I felt I understood the tea needs of a hotel and knew I spoke the language hotel food and beverage directors understood. Credibility statement in hand, I took myself straightaway to that grande dame of New York's hotels, the stately old Plaza, where tea had famously been served in the Palm Court since the hotel's opening in 1907, and made them a proposition. The result is available today as the Palm Court Blend, as rich and fine a tea blend as Bill MacMelville and I knew how to create, and a steady seller both at the Plaza and at Harney & Sons.

The Plaza was not our very first hotel account, but I was determined it should become one of our first among a great many others. By concentrating on hotels, I hoped to get fine teas before a sophisticated cross-section of Americans. Now, with almost three hundred major hotel accounts nationwide, it turns out we've succeeded doubly. Not only are thousands of people enjoying afternoon tea every day at hotels where oftentimes there was none before, but tens of thousands of people have learned to associate the pleasures of teatime at its best with Harney & Sons Fine Teas. Besides Ireland's St. Patrick, I also give thanks to those patron saints of tea, Lu Yu and Bodhidharma, who have abundantly blessed our undertaking.

The greatest blessing I've experienced in the tea business, however, is the chance to work alongside my sons Michael and Paul. Michael, who was the first to join me in 1987, left behind a promising career of his own in hotel management and took a serious cut in pay for several years in hopes his father's passion for tea was not a recipe for bankruptcy. In no time his own passion for tea was unsurpassable and his knowledge of tea has long since exceeded my own.

Fueled by Michael's energy and commitment, our little firm began to grow—and has kept on growing. By the time Paul joined our company in 1995, after serving as an officer in the Marines, we were fairly solvent and extremely optimistic about the future of tea in America and, therefore, of Harney & Sons Fine Teas.

But before continuing in the familiar vein of all proud fathers everywhere, let's get back to the subject at hand: cooking with tea.

Tea not only goes with food but also with friendship, socializing, and hospitality. This was the idea behind the first Harney Tea Summit in 1993. To that end, we invited to Salisbury a small group of our tea friends—Bill MacMelville, James Norwood Pratt, Dr. Mitch Gaynor and others—and a small group of media people from *Victoria, Gourmet,* the *New York Times,* and others. The idea was that we would all visit, eat, and drink Harney & Sons teas together while our tea friends taught our media friends a thing or two about it.

The group was so small we met in my living room and prepared all meals in our kitchen. This was the first time I deliberately set about impressing others with my cooking using tea. The tea-smoked salmon I served with a Lapsang Souchong beurre blanc won high praise, and I was sufficiently encouraged to repeat the summit the following year with more guests, a larger program and, of course, more food. Looking back, it's easy to see how quickly these things can get out of hand.

By 1997 the summit had morphed into the Harney Tea Conference with 232 paying attendees, not counting the growing number of participating friends in tea or the media. The meals, like the programs themselves, grew ever more extensive and elaborate. By 1998, when we realized we simply had to stop entertaining on this scale, these events had forced me to compose menus and test dishes and actually cook elbow to elbow with some of the most distinguished chefs and authors, including Eileen Yin-Fei Lo and Ellen Greaves of Takashimaya's Tea Box.

Merely to mention Joanna Pruess among great tea chefs is not sufficient, however. Without her as my co-author, all these explorations of cooking with tea would have remained not just a closed book but a nonexistent one!

Joanna and I have been friends since the day in 1986 when my son Keith (or was it my daughter Elyse?) showed me a *New York Times* article about an imaginative chef (then living in New Jersey) who cooked with tea. I phoned to introduce myself and offered to exchange recipes. I forget what I traded for Joanna's inspired Earl Grey reduction sauce, but that first recipe she provided me has been put to use at many a banquet since.

Joanna has presided over tastings for the annual Fancy Food Show for years and written regularly for the Sunday *New York Times Magazine,* the *Washington Post,* and many food magazines. Tea has been her constant companion throughout, as I happen to know, speaking as her tea purveyor, and a good deal of it has always found its way into her cooking. I believe nobody knows more about the use of different teas both to complement food and as ingredients in food.

Recipes Joanna has collected or that are of her own devising have been freely traded and widely imitated in our circle of friends and tea devotees for years. These are not recipes for the enjoyment of fine food alone, but also for good health and great living—all the things tea adds to civilized life. To keep them for ourselves alone would be, if not criminal, at least a violation of the very spirit of tea. And today, as when my passion for tea got me into the business years ago, I continue to promise great enjoyment to every lover of fine teas and fine foods who discovers Harney & Sons Fine Teas.

    —John Harney
      Salisbury, Connecticut, 2001

Love and scandal are the best sweeteners of tea.

—Henry Fielding, *Love in Several Masques*

Introduction

Ever since 2737 B.C. when, legend says, a few leaves from an overhead tea plant drifted into Emperor Shen Nung's cup of boiling water, tea has been considered a restorative and a source of well being. Far from being an apocryphal promise, many of tea's beneficial properties have been substantiated by modern medicine.

Dr. Mitchell Gaynor, director of the Weill Medical College in New York City, says both black and green teas boost the body's antioxidant capabilities and neutralize bacteria that cause dental cavities and gum disease. Additionally, oolong teas lower cholesterol, while green, white, and yellow teas (including gunpowder, Lung Ching, and sencha) diminish blood pressure levels. In a world fascinated with so-called nutriceuticals, tea is a leader.

Tea is also comforting. All ages are discovering anew the pleasures of a well-brewed cup of tea as part of a late afternoon meal or at home during any hour of the day or evening. But, that's not all.

Tea leaves also provide a lift of another sort in today's kitchens: as a stimulus to chefs and inventive cooks who are creating flavorful, stylish foods without added fat or cholesterol. You'll find tea-based vinaigrettes, sauces, and rubs used in many kitchens. Green tea ice cream is now available in many restaurants beyond Chinatown, as well as in some supermarkets. Chaice Cream (page 103), on the other hand, made with sweetened black Indian tea leaves spiced with cardamom and cinnamon and boiled with milk (a beverage known as chai) is every bit as tempting when frozen into ice cream. It may soon become your favorite dessert.

To the list of tea treats easily prepared at home, add Earl Grey–Chocolate Mousse (page 99) or Candied Ginger and Green Tea Bread (page 86). The bread, made with olive oil, green tea, and ginger, which aids digestion, is an indulgence that's easily forgiven.

There's more: a whole world more of tea-flavored cooking. Tea-Smoked Duck is an age-old Chinese classic, and the recipe for it is on page 57. So are marbleized thousand-year-old eggs. Devil those eggs, combine them with crab, and the results are a lively hors d'oeuvre strictly of today's vintage (see page 16).

Once you start experimenting with tea, it's like discovering a whole new world of cooking ingredients. Tea is magical. Use it to replace fats in some dishes, alcohol in others, as in the Tea'd Pan Sauce for steak on page 68. Your definition of seasonings will never be the same. Every category of food from snacks to desserts benefits from tea.

Yes, tea as a drink is still the most popular use for the leaves. For that reason, we've included a handful of beverages.

All of these recipes can be prepared with common home kitchen equipment. Most useful are an electric coffee or spice grinder to pulverize tea leaves, a kitchen brush to clean out the grinder, paper towels, and a couple of fine gauge strainers. A tea infuser is also helpful.

We've tested these dishes on our friends and families with great success. Along with those by Joanna Pruess and the Harney family, some noted tea experts and our friends have also sent along their favorites.

Throughout the text, the symbol ^H_T denotes a unique Harney tea blend. If you have a favorite or similar tea, of course it can be substituted. The symbol ✿ gives you useful tea information, such as why it's better to infuse tea before cooking with it rather than using the leaves. (Long boiling imparts the bitter taste of over-brewed tea.)

Finally, John Harney has suggested pairings of teas and food. Our choices of tea, as in other flavorings, are only a jumping-off point. Change them at will to please your own palate. And enjoy your own discovery of Old/New World tea recipes.

Eat Tea

The best quality tea must have creases like the leather boot of Tartar horsemen,
curl like the dewlap of a mighty bullock, unfold like a mist rising out of a ravine,
gleam like a lake touched by a zephyr, and be wet and soft like a
fine earth newly swept by rain.

Lu Yu, *Ch'a Ching*, the first book of tea, written at the beginning of the ninth century

Tea Essentials

A Tea Time Line

2737 B.C.
Leaves from an overhead tea plant drift into Emperor Shen Nung's cup of boiling water. The results were considered restorative and a source of well-being.

2000 B.C.
Watermelon is cultivated in Africa, figs in Arabia, tea and bananas in India, apples in the Indus Valley. Agriculture is well established in most of the central isthmus of the Western Hemisphere.

c.725 B.C.
In the Tang Dynasty, *ch'a*, tea in Chinese, is part of daily life.

222
Tea is mentioned as a substitute for wine for the first time in Chinese writings of the next half century.

708
Tea drinking gains popularity in China, where drinking the hot drink is safer than drinking unboiled, contaminated water. It is also valued for its alleged medicinal values.

805
Tea is introduced to Japan as a medicine. Saicho, a Buddhist bonze (priest), spends three years visiting Chinese Buddhist temples on orders from the emperor and returns with tea.

1191
Zen Buddhism is introduced to Japan by the priest Aeisai, who returns from a visit to China. Aeisai plants tea seeds, making medicinal claims for tea in 1214. Soon afterward, he publishes the first Japanese tea book.

1484
The tea ceremony is introduced by Japan's Yoshimasa. At age 48, the shogun encourages painting and drama. His reign was otherwise disastrous, but the tea ceremony will remain for centuries as a cherished part of Japanese culture.

1500
During the Ming Dynasty, the first teapots are made of clay taken from near Shanghai. They are

Basics of Tea

All tea comes from the same plant: the *Camellia sinensis.* How it is processed, however, determines the type of tea it will become.

There are four major types of teas—green, oolong, black, and black scented teas. In general, each estate and garden uses a single style of processing which is usually determined by geography, including elevation and moisture level, and farming practices.

Tea grows fastest at sea level to 6,500 feet in sandy or clay soil. The climate should be hot and moist—80 to 150 inches of rain annually with high humidity and fog. Tea also grows at higher elevations and in shaded areas but at a much slower rate. This climatic change also produces a more intense flavor tea, like Darjeeling. It is reasonably safe to say that Japan only produces green teas, Formosa (Taiwan) focuses on oolongs, and Ceylon and India produce primarily black teas.

Green Tea

China and Japan are the largest producers of green tea. Green tea is considered nonfermented, meaning the leaves are picked and allowed to dry in the sun in bamboo baskets for a few hours. The leaves are then pan-roasted and finally rolled into attractive shapes that provide pleasure from the leaf before, during, and after the tea is brewed. The leaves range in color from bright to dull green and are pliable.

Japanese green tea is steamed and processed into different forms, including powdered green tea or *matcha,* used even today for traditional Japanese tea ceremonies. In Japan there are three different grades of green tea: bancha, sencha, and gyokuro.

Bancha is Japan's ordinary green tea. It comes from the late summer pickings and is somewhat coarse in flavor and appearance. Sencha is the next grade up and comes from the first or second picking, or "flush," of a tea estate. The tea is steam fired and basket dried, and finally hand rolled. This process is more costly. Sencha gives off a grassy odor and is pale in color.

Harvested once a year, only the bud and tiny first leaf are plucked. The name means "precious dew."

Gyokuro is the highest grade of green tea. Due to the great amount of hand labor required, it is also the most expensive. This tea, once brewed, is a pale green to yellow color and has a clean, brisk flavor.

Oolong

Oolong tea is semifermented, partially withered and partially oxidized. China and Formosa (Taiwan) are the largest producers of this type of tea. Leaves used for oolong tea must be picked at precisely the right time and processed immediately afterwards. They are withered in direct sunlight, then shaken in bamboo baskets to bruise the edges of the leaves which turn a reddish brown color after oxidation has occurred. This bruising and drying of the leaves is repeated several times. Oolong teas are often referred to as brown tea because they are more oxidized than green teas, yet not as oxidized as black tea.

imitations of spouted wine earthenware. Oolong, black, and green teas predominate.

1591

Japanese tea master Rikyu Sen commits ritual suicide *(seppuku)* on orders from Toyotomi Hideyoshi. Sen had formalized the tea ceremony.

1597

The first English mention of tea appears in a translation of Dutch navigator Jan Hugo van Lin-Schooten's Travels. Van Lin-Schooten calls the beverage *chaa*.

1610

Tea arrives into Europe from Java courtesy of Dutch trading ships. The Amoy Chinese who sell it call it *tea* in their dialect.

1657

Public sale of tea begins in London as the East India Company undercuts Dutch prices and advertises tea as a panacea for apoplexy, catarrh, colic, consumption, drowsiness, epilepsy, gallstones, lethargy, migraine, paralysis, and vertigo. Tea is offered to Londoners at Thomas Garraway's coffee house in Exchange Alley between Cornhill and Lombard streets.

1658

The London periodical *Mercurius Politicus* carries an advertisement: "That excellent and by all Physitians approved China Drink called by the Chineans 'Tcha,' by other nations 'Tay,' alias 'Tea,' is sold at the Sultaness Head, a cophee-house in Sweeti Rents."

1662

Catherine da Braganza, after marrying Charles II, introduces the London court to the Lisbon fashion of drinking tea; she also introduces the Chinese orange.

1665

England imports less than 88 tons of sugar, a figure that will grow to 10,000 tons by the end of the century as tea consumption (encouraged by cheap sugar) increases in popularity.

1684

Tea sells on the Continent for less than 1 shilling per pound, but an import duty of 5 shillings per pound makes tea too costly for most Englishmen and encourages widespread smuggling. The English consume more smuggled tea than is brought in by orthodox routes.

1708
The United East India Company created by a merger of Britain's two rival East India companies is the strongest European power on the coasts of India. The company ships China tea as well as other goods, and it will pay regular dividends of 8 to 10 percent.

1712
The Rape of the Lock by Alexander Pope is a mock-heroic poem describing a day at Hampton Court where Queen Anne does "sometimes counsel take—and sometimes tea."

1717
A young London tea merchant, Thomas Twining, opens The Golden Lyon, a place where, unlike local coffee houses, women could enter to buy and drink tea.

1723
Robert Walpole reduces British duties on tea.

1767
The Townshend Revenue Act, passed by Parliament June 29, imposes duties on tea, glass, paint, oil, lead, and paper imported into Britain's American colonies in hopes of raising £40,000 per year.

A town meeting held at Boston to protest the Townshend Act adopts a nonimportation agreement.

1768
The East India Company imports 10 million pounds of tea per year into England.

1770
The Boston Massacre on March 5 leaves three dead, two mortally wounded, and six injured following a disturbance between colonists and British troops.

Parliament repeals the Townshend Revenue Act of 1767 in a bill passed April 12. Prime Minister North used his influence to have the act repealed.

Another important characteristic of oolong tea is that the leaf is never broken by rolling, like green tea, or by the machines used with black tea. The signature attribute of oolong is that the leaf is always long and whole.

Black Teas

Black teas vary considerably depending on the region and the way the tea is processed. There are two basic methods used in producing this fully fermented tea: the traditional method, which results in larger leaves with visual appeal and many variances, and what is known as the CTC method—Cut, Tear, and Curl. Machines cut, tear, and curl leaves after the withering stage to produce small, pellet-like pieces of tea that brew a strong cup of tea. Harney & Sons primarily uses the traditional method for their black teas but uses the CTC method in its blends.

There are four steps in producing a fully fermented tea. First the tea leaves must undergo full withering. Next they are rolled to discharge the chemicals within the leaf. Then the tea undergoes the oxidation or fermentation process. Finally, the leaf is fired to halt the breakdown and dried again to remove all moisture.

After the leaves are fermented they are graded. Grading refers to the size of the leaf only and is not a reflection of quality. Most grading terms refer only to black teas. They range from the smallest fannings, or tea dust, to the largest flowery orange pekoe (basic black) tea leaves. Green teas are usually graded by the name of the tea, gunpowder, for example.

Scented Teas

All of the above teas—green, oolong, and black—are used to make scented teas. During the blending process, the tea is mixed primarily with natural flavorings, oils, or flower petals, like roses or jasmine blossoms.

Types of Tea

There are more than 15,000 varieties of teas produced in about twenty-five counties of the world. With the diverse colors, sizes, and shape of tea leaves, as well as different methods for drying them, the taste of brewed tea can range from suble to pungent. The hue may also vary from pale yellow to vibrant red or robust mahogany brown. Below are some of the most popular varieties of tea.

Traditional-Style Teas

English Breakfast: 100% pure China Black (Keemun). It is strong and simple.

Earl Grey: A blend of four teas from China and India that has been infused with oil of bergamot, a rare citrus flavor from the Mediterranean.

Irish Breakfast: A strong tea made up of 100% Assam tea with a slightly malty flavor.

Darjeeling: Considered the queen of teas, grown high in the Himalayas. With a slight muscat flavor, it yields a light color in the cup and a fragrant "nose."

Orange Pekoe: A blend also referred to as Ceylon (Sri Lanka) and India, the two sources from which it comes. It is the basic black tea.

Lapsang Souchong: An unusual tea with large leaves smoked using a hand-fired method. It is a much loved tea with an intense smoky flavor.

Green and Oolong Teas

Gunpowder: From China, gunpowder takes its name from its hand-rolled pellet shape and leaden color. It steeps into a pale yellow liquid with an exquisite taste, and has one third the caffeine of black tea.

Moroccan Mint: Gunpowder green tea blended with aromatic peppermint leaves, producing a unique brisk green tea.

1773

The Tea Act, passed by Parliament on May 10, lightens duties on tea to give relief to the East India Company, which has seven years' supply in warehouses on the Thames and is being strained by storage charges.

The Tea Act permits tea to be shipped at full duty to the American colonies and to be sold directly to retailers, eliminating colonial middlemen and undercutting their prices.

Tea is left to rot on the docks at Charleston. New York and Philadelphia send tea-laden ships back to England.

"Two Letters on the Tea Tax" by John Dickinson are published in November.

Agitator Samuel Adams organizes the Boston Tea Party action with support from John Hancock, whose smuggling of contraband tea has been made unprofitable by the new measures.

The Boston Tea Party on December 16 demonstrates against the new English tea orders. Led by Lendall Pitts, scion of a Boston merchant family, a group of men, including Paul Revere, disguise themselves as Mohawks.

The Boston Tea Party Group board East India Company ships at Griffen's Wharf, and throw 342 chests of tea (valued at more than £9,650) from the London firm of Davison and Newman into Boston Harbor. Men of "sense and property" such as George Washington, deplore the Boston Tea Party.

1774

The British ship London docks at New York on April 22, and the Sons of Liberty prepare to follow the example set at Boston four months earlier. While making themselves up as Mohawks, an impatient crowd boards the vessel and heaves the tea into the Hudson.

Colonists at York, Maine, and Annapolis, Maryland, conduct tea parties like the one at Boston.

News of last year's Boston Tea Party reaches London in January via John Hancock's ship *Hayley.* Parliament passes coercive acts to bring the colonists to heel.

George III gives assent on March 31 to the Boston Port Bill and Boston harbor is closed on June 1 "until the East India Company shall have been reimbursed for its tea" and British authorities feel that trade can be resumed and duties collected.

1780

English sugar consumption reaches 12 pounds per year per capita, up from 4 in 1700, as Britons increase coffee and tea consumption.

1784

Parliament further lowers British import duties on tea. The lower duties end the smuggling that hurt the East India Company as the rewards become too small to justify the risks.

1790

Boston merchants start a triangular trade with clothing, copper, and iron to be bargained for furs. The sea captains will sell the cargoes at Canton and return round the Cape of Good Hope with Chinese porcelains, teas, and tiles.

1797

English tea consumption reaches an annual rate of 2 pounds per capita, a figure that increases fivefold in the next century.

1820

"Adulteration of Foods and Culinary Poisons" by English chemistry professor Frederick Accum enrages the vested interests. The book shows among other things that counterfeit China tea is made from dried thorn leaves colored with poisonous verdigris.

1823

Acting for the British government, Charles Bruce smuggles knowledgeable nationals out of China and puts them to work transplanting young tea bushes into nursery beds to begin tea plantations.

1824

Cadbury's Chocolate has its beginnings in a tea and coffee shop opened in Birmingham, England,

Citron Green: A wonderful introduction to green tea with a delicate citrus flavor and aroma and beautiful orange flowers.

Gyokuro: Japan's finest green tea. During the plucking season, the gardens are shaded to increase the bright green color of the leaves. Gyokuro has a bright green color, an intense vegetal flavor, and high levels of caffeine.

Sencha: From Japan, sencha is a clear, bright green tea with little caffeine. It is believed to have great health benefits.

Bancha: Also from Japan, bancha is the basic quality of green tea.

Herbal Teas (Caffeine-Free)

Chamomile: Egypt provides the finest chamomile, of which only the flower heads are used. Often referred to as sleepy-time tea, it is a tisane with definite body, and a fresh scent that is reminiscent of green apples.

Peppermint: A brisk drink made from dried peppermint leaves. It is a great stomach settler.

Raspberry: A blend of raspberry leaves, rose hips, orange peel, and hibiscus. It brews up into a ruby red color, and it cures everything, including the rainy day blues.

Passion Plum: An herbal infusion with the essences of cinnamon and plums that is heartier than most herbals.

Lemon Herbal: A blend of lemon grass and lemon peel that produces an herbal tea with a zesty lemon flavor. It is a light and soothing alternative to chamomile and an excellent bedtime tea.

Rooibos: This tea comes from just north of Cape Town, South Africa, where a relatively untouched resource called rooibos (redbush) lies. Reaching the United States only recently, it has become a favorite among tea drinkers because it is low in tannin, contains natural sweeteners, and is rich in essential minerals.

Lemon Verbena (*Verveine Odorante*): A traditional French herbal tisane. The green leaves produce a full-bodied herb tea with a lemony aroma that is perfect after dinner.

French *Tilleul*: Another traditional French herbal said to be a stress reliever. The leaves and flowers of the linden tree produce a light, subtle, woodsy brew. A cup of French tilleul is a soothing way to end a long day.

Elyse Harney Morris and John Harney

by John Cadbury who served an apprenticeship at Leeds and for bonded London tea houses. He employs a Chinese man to preside over his tea canister.

The Royal Navy reduces its daily rum ration from half a pint to a quarter pint, and tea becomes part of the daily ration.

1825

British colonists in Ceylon plant coffee bushes.

1826

The first tea to be retailed in sealed packages under a proprietary name is introduced by English Quaker John Horniman whose sealed, lead-lined packages have been designed in part to protect his tea from adulteration.

1830

Mormonism is founded by Joseph Smith. Their "Word of Wisdom" is a code of health prohibiting tea, coffee, alcohol, and tobacco.

Congress reduces U.S. duties on coffee, tea, salt, and molasses imports.

1831

Boston's S. S. Pierce Co. has its beginnings in a shop opened to sell "choice teas and foreign fruits" by local merchant Samuel Stillman Pierce.

1833

The East India Company loses its prized monopoly in the China trade (most of it in tea) by an act of the British prime minister Charles Grey, the second Earl Grey.

1837

Major Samuel Shaw barters cargo for $30,000 worth of tea and silk; the investors receive a 25 percent return on their capital. Shaw becomes first U.S. consul at Canton, and more Americans are encouraged to enter the China trade.

1839

Some 95 chests of Assam tea arrive at London and are sold at auction. Unlike green China tea, the leaves from India are fermented and the new black tea, less astringent than green tea, begins to gain popularity.

"Kingscote," a house built in 1839 on Bellevue Avenue, Newport, is acquired by William Henry King with money acquired in the tea trade and Newport becomes a favorite summer resort for the rich.

1840

Afternoon tea, introduced by Anna, the duchess of Bedford, is meant to quell 4 o'clock hunger as the dinner hour has moved closer to 7 or 8 o'clock. The tea interval will become a lasting British tradition, but the English still drink more coffee than tea.

1844

The Rochdale Society of Equitable Pioneers, the first modern cooperative society, opens a store in Toad Lane. Flour, oatmeal, butter, and sugar are its only initial wares but the store soon adds tea and groceries.

1849

Parliament abolishes Britain's Navigation Acts June 26, ending restrictions on foreign shipping. U.S. clipper ships are permitted to bring cargoes of China tea into British ports.

Harrods has its beginnings in a London grocery shop at 8 Brompton Road run by Philip Henry Burden. Tea wholesaler Henry Charles Harrod, of Eastcheap, takes over the shop that will grow to become one of the world's preeminent department stores.

1850

Tea catches up with coffee in popularity among the English.

The *Oriental,* the first U.S. clipper ship to be seen at London, arrives from Hong Kong after a 97-day voyage. It carries a 1,600-ton cargo of China tea and her $48,000 cargo fee nearly covers the cost of her construction.

British shipbuilders are inspired to copy the *Oriental*'s lines but are handicapped by English rules of taxation that consider length and beam in measuring tonnage while leaving depth untaxed.

The short, deep ships built at Aberdeen and on the Clyde do not approach the speed of the U.S. clipper ships, which soon abandon the China

The Correct Way to Brew Tea

1. Preheat a teapot by pouring boiling water into it, raising the temperature of the pot to 180°F.

2. Discard the water. For a teapot holding up to 6 cups, add 1 teaspoon of loose tea for each cup of tea you're brewing. For pots that hold up to 12 cups, add an extra teaspoon of tea "for the pot."

3. Pour fresh boiling water over the tea or tea bag. This super-saturates the tea, allowing the perfect extraction of the flavor.

4. For black tea, the water temperature should be 210°F, just under the boiling point. Let the tea steep for a full 5 minutes. Herbal teas also require near boiling water and should be steeped for 5 minutes. For green tea, use water below the boiling point—the temperature should be about 180 to 185°F. Steep for 3 minutes.

5. Pour tea through a strainer into a cup.

The Harney Method of Decaffeinating Tea

Since caffeine is the most water-soluble part of tea leaves—followed by color and flavor—tea is easily decaffeinated:

Pour hot water over the leaves. After 30 seconds, discard the water and pour fresh water over the leaves, then continue to steep for the proper length of time.

Some Guidelines for Using Tea in Cooking

1. Use fresh tea leaves that have been stored correctly, not old tea. It's preferable to buy small amounts of loose tea, rather than a whole box of tea bags, both because it is less expensive and because the flavor of loose tea is more intense. Tea bags contain so-called *fannings*, small particles of tea dust, left after the larger leaves are removed. They lose their flavor faster than loose tea.

2. Always use freshly brewed tea for cooking; leftover tea never adds good flavor to foods.

3. Once tea is brewed, strain and discard the leaves. Cook only with the tea liqueur unless using ground leaves as a part of the recipe.

4. Tea can be infused in other liquids than water, such as juice, stock, milk, and cream. Bring the liquid just to a boil (for black tea) and under the boil (for green tea and herbal teas).

5. The flavor of ground tea dissipates quickly. Pulverize only as much as needed for each recipe. Be sure to wipe out the grinder each time to prevent any residue from flavoring the next tea. A small kitchen brush helps to clean the inside of the grinder. Or grind a tablespoon of raw rice to powder in the grinder and discard it.

trade for the more profitable business of transporting gold seekers to California.

1851

The London Great Exhibition forbids sale of wine, spirits, beer, and other intoxicating beverages but permits tea, coffee, chocolate, cocoa, lemonade, ices, ginger beer, and soda water.

1855

A report of the Analytical Sanitary Commission of *The Lancet* is published at London. A. H. Hassall reports that all but the most costly food and tea contain trace amounts of arsenic, copper, lead, or mercury.

1856

The first tea plantations are planted in the Darjeeling Estates of northern India.

1859

The A&P retail food chain has its beginnings in the Great American Tea Company store opened at 31 Vesey Street, New York, by local merchant George Huntington Hartford, who persuaded his employer, George P. Gilman, to give up his hide and leather business.

Hartford and Gilman buy whole clipper ship cargoes in New York harbor, sell the tea at less than one third the price charged by other merchants, identify their store with flaked gold letters on a Chinese vermilion background, and start what will grow into A&P.

1861

U.S. tariffs rise as Congress passes the first of three Morrill Acts which boost tariffs to an average of 47 percent. Duties on tea, coffee, and sugar are increased as a war measure.

1863

The Great American Tea Company grows to six stores and begins selling a line of groceries in addition to tea.

1866

More than 90 percent of Britain's tea still comes from China.

The Great Tea Race from Foochow to London pits 11 clipper ships who race to minimize spoilage of the China tea in their hot holds. The voyage still takes close to 3 months.

1869
The 10-year-old Great American Tea Company is renamed the Great Atlantic and Pacific Tea Company, or A&P, to capitalize on the national excitement about the new transcontinental rail link.

Coffee rust, *Hamileia vastatrix,* appears in Ceylon plantations and spreads throughout the Orient and the Pacific in the next two decades. It destroys the coffee-growing industry. Soaring coffee prices lead to wide-scale tea cultivation.

The English clipper ship *Cutty Sark* sails for Shanghai to begin a 117-day voyage, with 28 crewmen to handle the 10 miles of rigging that control her 32,000 square feet of canvas. Built for the tea trade, the ship has a figurehead wearing a short chemise.

1871
Huntington Hartford of A&P sends emergency rail shipments of tea and coffee to Chicago, where grocery stores were burnt in the great October fire. When the city is rebuilt, Hartford opens A&P stores.

1872
A strict Adulteration of Food, Drink and Drugs Act amends Britain's 1860 pure food laws, making the sale of adulterated drugs a punishable crime and making it an offense to sell a mixture containing ingredients added to increase weight without advising the customer.

1875
A new British Sale of Food and Drugs Law tightens restrictions against adulteration, making any adulteration injurious to health punishable with a heavy fine and making a second offense punishable with imprisonment.

1876
Grocer Thomas J. Lipton opens his first shop Glasgow at age 26. Lipton sailed to America at age 15 to spend four years learning the merchandising methods employed in the grocery section of a New York department store.

1879
The Cup of Tea is painted by Mary Cassatt.

Uses for Tea in Cooking

This small book is meant to show you some of the ways, both traditional and contemporary, in which tea can be used in cooking. Once you begin experimenting, you will discover, as I did, that using tea is like discovering a whole new range of spices and herbs.

We hope the book tempts you, gives you some preliminary guidelines, and piques your imagination about the many places a pinch of tea can add excitement to your cooking.

Tea can be used:

- As an infusion to thin down or add flavor to other liquids
- As a replacement for oil or other liquids
- As a marinade
- As a simmering or braising liquid
- Powdered as a flavoring in foods
- Powdered as a coating or rub
- As whole leaves for smoking
- As a coloring agent
- As a decorative garnish

Seven Cardinal Sins that Result in Inferior Tea for Drinking or Cooking

1. **Poor Purchasing.** "A good pot of tea cannot be made from bad tea," says John Harney. You must purchase a high quality, non-stale tea that's been stored properly.

2. **Mixture of Flavors.** Tea is like a blotter—it picks up off flavors and so should be brewed only in pots used for making tea.

3. **Using Inferior Water or Water at Incorrect Temperatures.** Water temperature is critical for great tea; it should be pure spring water to avoid chemical tastes and it must be just at boiling for black teas and just under boiling for green teas and herbals to extract good tea flavor.

4. **Using an Insufficient Amount of Tea.** Too much loose tea is better than too little. A teaspoon per cup for smaller pots is appropriate. For pots of 8 to 12 cups, an extra teaspoon for the pot is good. When brewed for the proper time, if the tea is too strong, it can be diluted to the desired strength.

1880
More than 95 A&P grocery stores are scattered across America from Boston to Milwaukee; the Great Atlantic & Pacific Tea Co. will not have a store on the West Coast for another 50 years.

1884
Ceylon's coffee output falls to 150,000 bags, down from 700,000 in 1870, when the rust disease caused by *Hamileia vastatrix* begins making deep inroads. The last shipment of coffee beans leaves the island in 1899.

1889
Rust finishes off Ceylon's coffee industry. Demand increases for Latin American coffee.

1890
Thomas Lipton enters the tea business to assure supplies of tea at low cost for his three hundred grocery shops. He offers "The Finest the World Can Produce" at 1 shilling 7 pence a pound when the going price is roughly a shilling higher.

1893
Lipton registers a new trademark for the tea he has been selling since 1890, which is sold only in packages. Over the facsimile signature *Thomas J. Lipton, Tea Planter, Ceylon,* Lipton prints the words "Nongenuine without this signature."

1897
Britons begin to eat lunch, dooming the classic British breakfast.

1898
Annual British tea consumption averages 10 pounds per capita, up from 2 pounds in 1797.

1899
English tea magnate Thomas Lipton has the racing yacht *Shamrock* I built for the first of five efforts he will make to regain the America's Cup, but the U.S. defender *Columbia* defeats Lipton's boat 3 to 0.

1902
Barnum's Animal Crackers are introduced by the National Biscuit Co., which controls 70 percent of U.S. cracker and cookie output. It joins the line of Nabisco products that include Social Tea Biscuits.

1904

Tea bags are pioneered by New York tea and coffee shop merchant Thomas Sullivan who sends samples of his various tea blends to customers in small hand-sewn muslin bags. Finding that they can brew tea simply by pouring boiling water over a tea bag in a cup, customers place hundreds of orders for Sullivan's tea bags, which are soon packed by a specially developed machine.

Green tea and Formosa tea continue to outsell black tea five to one in the United States.

Iced tea is reputedly created at the St. Louis fair by English tea concessionaire Richard Blechynden, when he observes sweltering fair goers passing him by. Evidence is produced of prior invention.

1909

Thomas Lipton begins blending and packaging his tea in New York. His U.S. business will be incorporated in 1915, and three years after his death in 1931, his picture will begin appearing on the red-and-yellow packages that identify Lipton products.

1912

A new Filene's with a seven-foot doorman opens in Boston on September 3 at the corner of Washington and Summer Streets in a building designed by Daniel Burnham. Edward Filene will hold free tea dances.

1913

Swann's Way (Du Côte de chez Swann) is written by French novelist Marcel Proust whose memories of childhood have been revived by tasting shell-shaped madeleine cakes dipped in tea.

1918

British food rationing begins with sugar January 1 and is extended in February to include meat, butter, and margarine. Other rationed commodities include 4 ounces of jam and 2 ounces of tea (weekly).

5. **Using Cold Teapots or Infusers.** A teapot must be heated before putting in the tea, otherwise the teapot will absorb the heat and prevent the extraction of tea flavors at the crucial time. There is a 25-degree difference between heated and unheated pots within the first three minutes.

6. **Pouring the Tea before It Is Ready.** Tea must steep for its full designated time before the intense tea flavor is extracted. Caffeine comes off first, then color, and finally flavor. Pouring too soon will result in good color but poor flavor.

7. **Timing Tea by Color.** With so many varieties of tea in the world, produced in so many countries, there are many different shades of tea. Do not judge the brew time of tea by color—use a clock. Oversteeped tea tastes bitter.

Tea Storage

Three things cause tea to deteriorate:

Moisture does the worst damage; therefore, tea should always be stored in an airtight container that won't allow moisture to reach the tea. This also prevents tea from being contaminated by the flavors and aromas of nearby food.

Sunlight also causes the quality of tea to decline. Store tea in an opaque container since light will turn the tea leaf grey.

Type of tea leaf also makes a difference. The tighter the roll of the leaf—like gunpowder green with its leaves rolled into tiny balls—the longer the shelf life. Generally, flavored tea has the shortest shelf life, followed by green, oolong, and then black tea. It is recommended that green tea be stored in the refrigerator. Never store tea in the freezer.

1953
White Rose Redi-Tea, introduced by New York's Seeman Brothers, is the world's first instant iced tea.

1983
John Harney opens Harney & Sons Tea Company, Salisbury, Connecticut.

Always drink tea like it was life itself, without wasting the aroma.
Never drink more than three cups: Tea is the very essence of moderation.

Lu Yu, *Ch'a Ching,* the first book of tea

Hors d'Oeuvres and First Courses

Thousand-Year-Old Deviled Eggs and Crab
Teasy Spiced Pecans
Caper, Shallot and Green Tea Cream Cheese
Lapsang Souchong Gravlax
Savory Swirls
Green Tea Dumplings
Tea's Toasts
Pear, Gorgonzola, and Watercress Salad
Oolong Boiled Shrimp
Shredded Chicken Salad with Asian Peanut Dressing
Squid, Asparagus, and Bell Pepper Salad with Lemon Verbena Aioli
Butternut Squash Soup
Hearty Wild Mushroom–Barley Soup

Thousand-Year-Old
Deviled Eggs and Crab

Makes 12 half eggs

And you thought deviled eggs were old hat! This is a traditional Chinese appetizer but our version is up-to-the-minute. The marble pattern intensifies the longer the shelled eggs are exposed to air.

6 eggs
4 Darjeeling or other black tea tea bags
2 tablespoons soy sauce
6 ounces crabmeat, picked over and flaked
¼ cup minced shallots
2 tablespoons minced pickled ginger
1 tablespoon pickled ginger liquid
Pinch of powdered wasabi or dab of paste wasabi
6 tablespoons mayonnaise, regular or reduced-fat
½ + teaspoon rice wine vinegar
Salt and white pepper
Slices of pickled ginger, for garnish
Chives, cut into 1-inch lengths, for garnish

1. Put the eggs in a saucepan and cover with water. Bring just to a boil, then reduce the heat and gently simmer for 10 minutes. Lift out eggs with a slotted spoon and set aside. When cool enough to handle, gently roll them on a counter to crack the shells all over. Do not peel.

2. Meanwhile, bring 3 cups of water to a boil, add the tea bags and soy sauce, and steep for 5 minutes. Discard the tea bags, squeezing to extract as much liquid as possible. Place the eggs in the liquid, simmer gently for 10 minutes, then refrigerate for 6 to 8 hours in the liquid.

3. Drain the eggs, peel, and blot dry. Let them stand for at least 1 hour (or longer in the refrigerator) for the marbled pattern to develop. Carefully cut the eggs in half lengthwise, and remove and mash the yolks. Combine the yolks with the crabmeat, shallots, and minced pickled ginger. Blend the pickled ginger liquid, wasabi, mayonnaise, and vinegar together, then combine this with the crab mixture. Season to taste with salt and pepper.

4. Fill each egg half with a rounded mound of the crab mixture. Top with a small slice of pickled ginger and a piece of chive.

Thousand-year-old deviled eggs and crab.

Teasy Spiced Pecans

Makes 4 cups

You can spend lots of money on fancy snacks, but few will compare with the taste of these nuts and the bravos that will follow when your guests sample this nibble. ✪ Vary the tea and spices to create your own signature blend. Other nuts or a mixture of nuts will work well also.

> 1 teaspoon vegetable oil
> 1 egg white
> ¼ cup sugar
> 2 tablespoons Hot Cinnamon Spice or other
>   cinnamon-scented tea leaves, finely ground
> ½ teaspoon salt
> Pinch of ground white pepper
> ¾ pound pecan halves

1. Preheat the oven to 350°F. Oil a large, flat baking pan or cookie sheet.
2. Beat the egg white in a deep bowl until frothy. Combine the sugar, tea, salt, and pepper in another bowl. Add the pecans to the egg white, turning to coat evenly. Transfer to the second bowl and toss to cover with the sugar mixture.
3. Distribute the nuts evenly on the pan and bake for 15 minutes. Remove, turning with a spatula as they cool. When completely cool, store in an airtight container.

Caper, Shallot, and Green Tea Cream Cheese

Makes ½ cup

Cream cheese blended with green tea, capers, and minced shallots makes an aromatic dip for vegetables or a spread for sandwiches, like a wrap of ham or smoked turkey, Muenster cheese, and thinly sliced sweet onions. Or spread it over prosciutto and wrap it around pencil-thin asparagus spears.

½ cup whipped cream cheese, regular or low-fat
2 teaspoons green tea leaves, finely ground
2 teaspoons small capers, drained and rinsed
½ tablespoon hot water, or more as needed
2 tablespoons minced shallots

Combine the cream cheese, tea, capers, and ½ tablespoon hot water in an electric blender and purée until smooth, adding just enough additional water to smooth out the mixture. Scrape it into a small bowl, stir in the shallots, cover, and refrigerate until needed. Serve chilled.

Lapsang souchong gravlax.

Lapsang Souchong Gravlax

Serves at least 6 for hors d'oeuvres

In Scandinavia, gravlax is traditionally cured with salt, sugar, and dill. In our contemporary version, smoky Lapsang souchong tea leaves and Chinese five-spice powder infuse a complex flavor that enhances salmon's sweet taste. To add to the Asian theme, serve the gravlax on crunchy sesame rice cakes, then drizzle with a little lime juice. Thinner pieces of salmon from the tail cure faster and are easier to cut than center-cut steaks. Try to match two tail pieces of about equal size. ✿ Try lemon verbena tea leaves for dill-cured salmon. They add a subtle twist to the taste.

1 ½ **cups coarsely chopped cilantro**
1 ½ **pounds fresh salmon fillet, cut into 2 equal pieces**
2 **tablespoons coarse salt**
1 ½ **tablespoons sugar**
1 **tablespoon Lapsang souchong tea leaves, lightly crumbled**
1 ½ **teaspoons Chinese five-spice powder**
1 **tablespoon mirin**
Lime juice, to drizzle on gravlax (optional)
Crunchy crackers, for serving

1. Sprinkle about one third of the cilantro in the bottom of a deep glass or other nonreactive dish large enough to hold the salmon fillet flat. Lay 1 fillet, skin side down, in the dish.
2. Combine the salt, sugar, tea, and Chinese five-spice powder and sprinkle over the fish. Cover with another third of the cilantro. Drizzle with the mirin and place the remaining salmon, skin side up, over the first fillet. Scatter with the remaining cilantro. Cover the dish with plastic wrap and place a plate or dish with two 8- to 12-ounce cans on it to weight it evenly.
3. Refrigerate for 48 to 72 hours, turning and basting every 12 hours, until the flesh no longer appears translucent. Once cured, remove the fish from dish, scrape off the cilantro and spice mixture, and pat dry. Thinly slice the salmon on the diagonal, working from the tip of the tail. Drizzle with a little lime juice, if desired, and serve on crunchy crackers.

Savory Swirls

Makes about 4 dozen

Here's another cocktail offering that's sure to draw raves from your guests. These small, flaky pastries swirled with a layer of Irish Breakfast tea and sautéed onions are heavenly.

>   2 tablespoons olive oil
>   1 ¼ cups finely chopped onions
>   2 tablespoons Irish Breakfast tea leaves
>   2 to 3 tablespoons chicken or vegetable stock
>   1 teaspoon Worcestershire sauce
>   1 teaspoon salt
>   Freshly ground black pepper
>   8 ounces frozen all-butter puff pastry, defrosted
>   according to package directions

1. Heat the olive oil in a large skillet over medium-high heat until hot. Add the onions and sauté just until golden brown, 6 to 8 minutes, then scrape them into an electric blender. Add the tea, 2 tablespoons of stock, the Worcestershire sauce, salt, and pepper to taste and purée until smooth, adding more stock if necessary to smooth out the mixture. Set aside.

2. Lightly flour a work space and rolling pin. Roll the pastry into a 6 X 18-inch rectangle, then brush off any excess flour. Working with the long side horizontal, spread the onion-tea mixture over the rectangle, leaving a 1-inch border at the uppermost edge. Starting with the bottom long edge, roll up the pastry jelly-roll fashion, gently pressing the top edge to seal. Carefully wrap in plastic wrap, gently flattening the roll slightly so the spirals are oval shaped. Refrigerate the pastry on a cookie sheet until firm, at least 2 hours. (This may be done up to 4 days ahead of time.)

3. Preheat oven to 375°F. Line 1 or 2 cookie sheets with parchment paper.

4. Remove the pastry from the refrigerator. Using a sharp knife, cut the roll crosswise into ⅜-inch slices. Place the slices on the parchment, leaving 1 inch space between them.

5. Bake in the middle of the oven until the tops are lightly browned, 11 to 15 minutes. If using 2 pans, rotate the pans during baking for even cooking. Turn each swirl with a spatula and bake until the second side is lightly browned and the centers are cooked through, 6 to 8 minutes. Remove the pans, slide the swirls onto a rack to cool, and continue until all swirls are baked. Store in a container with a loose-fitting lid.

Green Tea Dumplings

Makes about 60 dumplings

Chef Danny Lee, our favorite Chinese cooking expert (and CIA professor) prepares these dumplings to great acclaim. He uses green tea in both the dough and the filling and serves the dumplings with a traditional dipping sauce.

Dumpling Dough

2 ¼ cups hot water
1 tablespoon finely ground green tea leaves
1 tablespoon sugar
2 pounds all-purpose flour

Filling

1 ½ pounds ground pork
1 ½ pounds napa cabbage, cored and finely chopped
1 egg, beaten
3 tablespoons finely chopped scallions, including green parts
2 tablespoons green tea leaves, finely chopped (see Note)
1 tablespoon minced fresh ginger
1 tablespoon salt, or more as needed
1 teaspoon ground white pepper
½ cup soy sauce
2 tablespoons sesame oil
Sesame oil, for frying (optional)
Dumpling Dipping Sauce (recipe follows)

1. To make the dough, combine the water, tea, sugar, and flour in a large bowl and mix into a smooth dough. Gather into a ball, cover, and let rest for 30 minutes.
2. To make the filling, while the dough is resting, combine the pork, cabbage, egg, scallions, tea leaves, ginger, salt, pepper, soy sauce, and sesame oil together in a large bowl and mix well. Cook a small amount of the filling in a skillet to check the seasonings.
3. Cut the dough into ½-ounce portions, and roll each out on a floured board into a 5-inch circle.

4. Place 1 tablespoon of the filling on one half of each piece of dough. Fold the other half over and crimp the edges together.
5. Boil the dumplings in salted water for 8 minutes and drain on paper towels. If desired, heat a little sesame oil in a large skillet. When hot, cook the dumplings until brown on both sides, turning once. Serve the dumplings with the dipping sauce.

Note: If the green tea leaves are very dry, soak them in warm water for 5 minutes before chopping.

Dumpling Dipping Sauce
Makes 1 cup

½ cup chicken stock
¼ cup Japanese soy sauce
1 tablespoon minced garlic
1 tablespoon minced scallions
1 tablespoon sesame oil
1 teaspoon hot bean paste, available at Asian markets
    and some supermarkets
1 teaspoon sugar
Chopped cilantro, to garnish (optional)

Stir all of the ingredients together and pass with the dumplings.

Tea's Toasts

Makes 24

Here's a pair of tempting hors d'oeuvres bites. The different cheeses and teas make them distinct: Number I is subtly nutty and smoky; number II is more herbaceous. Serve both together, but allow them to cool a minute or two to let the flavors come through. Or spread either mixture on sandwich-size bread for a delicious open-faced treat.

Tea's Toasts I
1 cup (4 ounces) finely shredded Gruyère or other Swiss cheese
¼ cup (about 1 ounce) grated imported Parmesan cheese
2 tablespoons minced shallots
1 tablespoon Earl Grey tea leaves, finely ground
3 tablespoons mayonnaise, regular or reduced-fat
12 cocktail-size slices European-style whole-grain dark
    pumpernickel bread

Tea's Toasts II
1 cup (4 ounces) finely shredded sharp Cheddar cheese
¼ cup toasted fresh bread crumbs
1 tablespoon green tea leaves, finely ground
3 tablespoons mayonnaise, regular or reduced-fat
12 cocktail-size slices Danish-style light rye bread

1. Turn on a small toaster oven or conventional oven to broil. Lay the bread slices on a pan or cookie sheet.
2. For Tea's Toasts I, combine both cheeses, shallots, tea, and mayonnaise together in a bowl. Spread on the pumpernickel bread, patting to smooth. Broil until the cheese is hot and bubbling, watching that the cheese doesn't burn. Remove and serve.
3. For Tea's Toasts II, combine the cheese, bread crumbs, tea, and mayonnaise together in a bowl. Spread on the light rye bread, patting to smooth. Broil until the cheese is hot and bubbling, watching that it doesn't burn. Remove and serve.

Pear, Gorgonzola, and watercress salad with savory swirls (page 22).

Pear, Gorgonzola, and Watercress Salad

Serves 4

This appealing salad's tea vinaigrette plays well against the sweet pears and tangy Gorgonzola cheese. Chèvre would also be an excellent cheese to use with the pears. The recipe was suggested by Linda Dannenberg, the author of *Perfect Vinaigrettes* and many books on French cooking and baking. She used Birthday Tea from Mariage Frères, the French tea emporium. Fragrant Earl Grey tea or oolong are other fine choices.

Tea Vinaigrette

1 rounded teaspoon tea leaves of choice in a tea ball or 1 tea bag
⅓ cup white wine vinegar
2 tablespoons honey
1 teaspoon chopped thyme leaves
1 teaspoon minced shallots
Fine sea salt
Freshly ground black pepper
1 cup sunflower or canola oil

Pear, Gorgonzola and Watercress Salad

4 ounces mixed baby lettuces
6 ounces watercress, coarse stems removed
2 ripe red Bartlett pears, cored and cut lengthwise into thin slices
4 ounces Gorgonzola cheese, crumbled
Freshly ground black pepper

1. To make the vinaigrette, combine the tea and vinegar in a very small saucepan and bring to a boil over high heat. Lower the heat and simmer for 1 minute. Remove the pan from the heat and set aside, allowing the tea to steep in the vinegar until cooled. Remove the tea ball or tea bag and gently squeeze the bag or leaves to extract as much vinegar as possible into the pot.

2. Transfer the vinegar to a glass or stainless steel bowl. Add the honey, thyme, shallots, a pinch of salt, and

several turns of ground pepper and whisk until blended and smooth. Continuing to whisk, gradually add the oil in a slow, steady stream until blended. The mixture will not emulsify. Transfer to a jar, cover tight-ly, and refrigerate for at least 4 hours before serving. Stored tightly covered in the refrigerator, the vinaigrette will keep for 2 weeks.

3. To prepare the salad, divide the field greens among 4 salad plates. Add the watercress and the pear slices radiating, like spokes, from the center of each plate. Sprinkle the cheese over the salad, mainly in the center. Spoon the vinaigrette over the salad, adding several grinds of pepper, and serve.

Oolong Boiled Shrimp

Serves 3 to 4

Along Maine's coastline, you sometimes find sweet fresh shrimps that are only an inch long. I first tasted them in Northeast Harbor. They're either boiled in their shells or peeled just before a brief cooking, then served with melted butter. A spoonful of oolong tea leaves added to the water imparts a subtle richness to their sweet taste. Butter swirled with a dash of soy sauce and minced garlic make this an easy and delicious first course, perhaps on lettuce-lined plates, or an hors d'oeuvre served with toothpicks. ✿ Because oolong tea leaves are large, they are readily removed even at table. If you prefer, brew a strong oolong tea, strain and cook as described.

> 4 to 6 tablespoons unsalted butter
> 1 small clove garlic, minced
> Few dashes of soy sauce
> Kosher or coarse sea salt
> 1 tablespoon oolong tea leaves
> 1 pound small Maine shrimp, peeled just before cooking
> ¼ cup thinly sliced scallions, including green parts

1. Melt the butter in a small saucepan. Turn off the heat, add the garlic and soy sauce, and set aside.
2. Fill a large, deep skillet with water. Add the sea salt and tea leaves and bring to a full boil. Add the shrimp, turn off the heat, and let sit until pale pink and just opaque. The shrimps cook within minutes. Drain, transfer to a bowl. Pick off tea leaves, if desired. Toss with the garlic butter and scallions, and serve.

Shredded Chicken Salad with Asian Peanut Dressing

Serves 4

Leftover chicken, shredded, and your choice of vegetables are transformed into an easy main course salad with this Asian-flavored peanut dressing. It's easily doubled so you'll have enough keep to keep in the refrigerator to drizzle over seared shrimp, skewered beef, steamed vegetables, or Asian noodles. ✿ Brewed black tea (your choice: from smoky Lapsang souchong to simple English Breakfast) adds flavor and moisture to sauces without the calories and fat of oils.

Asian Peanut Dressing

½ cup peanut butter, smooth or chunky
½ cup coarsely chopped cilantro
1 piece fresh ginger, about ¾ inch long
½ cup brewed black tea
2 tablespoons rice wine vinegar
1½ to 2 tablespoons soy sauce
2 tablespoons sugar
Chinese hot chili oil, as needed, available at many
    Asian markets and supermarkets

Chicken Salad

1 head romaine lettuce, separated into leaves
2 cups finely shredded cooked chicken
Salt and freshly ground black pepper
1 red bell pepper, cut into fine julienne
6 ounces sugar snap peas, strings removed and blanched until crisp-tender
1 cup thinly sliced scallions, including green parts
2 tablespoons lightly toasted sesame seeds, for garnish

1. To make the dressing, combine the peanut butter, cilantro, ginger, tea, vinegar, soy sauce, and sugar in a blender and purée until smooth, scraping down the sides of the jar as needed. Add chili oil to taste. Refrigerate until needed.

2. To prepare the salad, line a salad bowl with the large romaine leaves. Cut the remaining leaves crosswise into 1-inch pieces and add to the bowl. Mix the chicken with about ½ cup of the peanut sauce, season with salt, if needed, and pepper, and mound the chicken on the lettuce. Arrange the bell pepper around the chicken, scatter with the snap peas, and sprinkle with the scallions. Drizzle about 3 to 4 tablespoons of the remaining peanut sauce over the salad, sprinkle with the sesame seeds, and serve.

Squid, asparagus, and bell pepper salad with lemon verbena aioli.

Squid, Asparagus, and Bell Pepper Salad with Lemon Verbena Aioli

Serves 4 as a first course or light main course

You'll discover a whole new dimension to squid with these fork-tender rings blended with colorful chunks of asparagus and red bell pepper. Aioli—traditionally a lemony-garlic mayonnaise—is enlivened with the scent of lemon verbena tea. Use the same sauce on steamed asparagus or artichokes.

Lemon Verbena Aioli

¼ cup light cream or half-and-half
2 teaspoons crushed lemon verbena tea leaves
1 egg yolk
1 teaspoon minced garlic
2 tablespoons fresh lemon juice
1 teaspoon Dijon mustard
¾ cup vegetable oil
Salt and white pepper

Squid Salad

1 pound cleaned squid
¾ pound young asparagus, woody stalks removed
1 large red bell pepper, cut into medium dice
1 cup thinly sliced scallions, including green parts
Salt and freshly ground black pepper
Juice of ½ lemon, as needed
Romaine leaves, for garnish (optional)

1. To prepare the aioli, bring the light cream just to a simmer, stir in the lemon verbena tea, remove from the heat, and infuse for about 1 hour. Then strain, pressing to extract as much liquid as possible. Meanwhile, combine the egg yolk, garlic, lemon juice, and mustard in an electric blender and blend well. Scrape down the sides. With the motor running, begin adding the oil in little drops until the egg begins to emulsify. Once it starts to thicken, add the oil in a slow, steady stream. When all the oil is

added, add the tea-infused cream, season with salt and pepper, scrape the aioli into a clean bowl, and set aside.

2. To make the salad, bring a large skillet of cold water to a simmer. Add the squid and cook gently just until it turns white, about 45 seconds. Remove, drain, blot dry, and cut into 3/4-inch rings. Steam or boil the asparagus until crisp-tender, drain, and blot dry. Cut diagonally into 3/4-inch slices and combine with the squid, bell pepper, and scallions in a large bowl.

3. Toss the salad with the aioli. Season to taste with salt and pepper. Add lemon juice, as needed, and serve at once or refrigerate until later. The salad can be made up to 1 day ahead and chilled.

4. Line 4 plates with romaine leaves, divide the squid salad among the plates, and serve.

Butternut Squash Soup

Serves 4

"Ambrosial" is how friends described this velvety soup with its subtle sweetness, thanks to unsweetened applesauce, and its smokiness from Lapsang souchong tea. Once the squash is tender, the soup takes just minutes to make. Oven-roasting makes the vegetable sweeter than either boiling or cooking it in a microwave oven, and it's worth the extra time. ✡ When you don't want extra salt to season foods, grinding tea leaves with an equal amount of dry white bread crumbs turns the mixture into a powdery, spice-like consistency that's easily sprinkled on as a seasoning just before serving.

> **2 pounds butternut squash, split and seeds removed**
> **1 teaspoon oil**
> **2½ cups chicken stock**
> **2 tablespoons Lapsang souchong tea leaves**
> **⅔ cup unsweetened applesauce**
> **Salt and white pepper**
> **1 teaspoon Lapsang souchong tea leaves**
> **1 teaspoon dry fresh white bread crumbs**

1. Preheat the oven to 350°F.
2. Brush both halves of the squashes with oil and bake, cut side down, until completely tender, about 45 minutes. Remove and when cool enough to handle, scrape the squash into an electric blender or food processor. You should have about 2 cups of squash.
3. While the squash cooks, bring the chicken stock to a boil. Pour it over the 2 tablespoons tea leaves, steep 5 minutes, then strain the liquid into a bowl, pressing to extract as much flavor as possible.
4. Add the applesauce and tea-infused stock to the blender bowl and purée until smooth. Season to taste with salt and pepper and scrape the mixture back into a clean saucepan and heat until hot.
5. Grind the 1 teaspoon tea leaves with the bread crumbs into a fine powder. Ladle the soup into 4 heated bowls, sprinkle a little tea powder in the center to garnish, and serve.

Hearty Wild Mushroom–Barley Soup

Serves 6 to 8

If the butternut squash soup on page 35 is subtle, this one's hardly mild-mannered. Woodsy mushrooms soaked in tea make this classic soup even heartier. The lemon juice really brings out the taste of the tea. A dollop of sour cream wouldn't hurt, but try the soup without the extra fat. You'll be pleased. Serve with a crusty baguette. ✿ To brew strong tea, add more tea leaves rather than steeping it beyond its designated time, which will make it bitter.

> 2 tablespoons gunpowder or Lapsang souchong leaves
> 1 ounce dried porcini or other wild mushrooms (2 cups loosely packed dried mushrooms)
> 1 cup pearl barley
> 1 tablespoon olive oil
> 2 large onions, chopped
> 8 ounces button, shiitake, or other fresh mushrooms, trimmed and sliced
> 5 cups beef stock
> 2 tablespoons tomato paste
> ½ teaspoon dried thyme leaves
> 1 tablespoon Worcestershire sauce
> 1 tablespoon lemon juice
> Salt and freshly ground black pepper
> ½ cup thinly sliced scallions, including green parts, for garnish

1. Bring 1 cup of water to a boil. Pour it over the tea leaves and steep for 3 minutes for gunpowder or 5 minutes for Lapsang souchong. Strain, pressing to extract as much liquid as possible. Pour the tea over the porcini and soak until softened, about 20 minutes. Strain the soaking liquid through a fine strainer lined with a dampened paper towel and reserve. Remove any sand or rough spots on the mushrooms, rinse, then coarsely chop.

2. Meanwhile, cook the barley in boiling water for 30 minutes, drain, rinse with cold water, and set aside. The barley will not be completely tender.

3. Heat the oil in a medium saucepan over high heat until hot. Add the onions and stir a couple of times. When they start to brown, about 5 minutes, cover the pan, turn the heat to medium-low, and sweat them until soft, about 5 minutes more.

4. Return the heat to high, add both the dried and the fresh mushrooms to the onions, and cook until they soften, 2 to 3 minutes, stirring occasionally. Blend the stock and tomato paste with the soaking liquid and add to the pot along with the barley. Bring the liquid to a boil, reduce the heat to a simmer, stir in the thyme, and cook until the barley is tender, about 25 minutes. Add the Worcestershire sauce, lemon juice, salt and pepper to taste, and simmer a few minutes more. Ladle into bowls, garnish with scallions, and serve.

[M]y mother explains . . . if I buy the cheap tea, then I am saying that my whole life has not been worth something better . . . If I buy just a little, then I am saying that lifetime is almost over, so she bought enough tea for another lifetime.

Amy Tan, *The Kitchen God's Wife*

Main Courses

Cold Lobster Tails with Green Tea—Sumac Mayonnaise
Broiled Bluefish with Green Tea Salt
Poached Scallops with Red Peppers and Vanilla Tea Vinaigrette
Earl Grey—Crusted Salmon
Black and White Sesame—Crusted Sole
Harney's Cinnamon Spice Tea—Smoked Swordfish Steaks
Seared Tuna and Fennel over Jasmine Rice
Whole Tea-Smoked Chicken
Baked Indian Chicken Breasts
Peach and Ginger—Glazed Chicken Legs
Breast of Duck with Curried Dried Fruit Chutney
Szechuan Tea—Smoked Duck
Tea-Smoked Quail over Spinach
Tastea Turkey Meat Loaf
Sautéed Pork Chops with Apricot—Wild Mushroom Glaze
Spicy-Smoky Baked Spareribs
Seared Steak with Tea'd Pan Sauce
Slowly Braised Lamb Shanks

Cold Lobster Tails with Green Tea–Sumac Mayonnaise

Serves 8 as a first course, 4 as a main course

As green tea moves into the mainstream of cooking, it's turning up in many new preparations and condiments. Ann Wilder, the queen of spice purveyors, combines green tea with sumac in her blend for Vann's Spices. We use it blended with some mayonnaise and scallions for split, cold poached lobster. They make a splendid summer meal or, using just the tail, an elegant first course. For warm lobsters, blend the spice rub with softened butter, rolling it into a log, chill, and then top the crustaceans with a generous slice of the flavorful butter.

> 1 cup prepared mayonnaise
> 2 tablespoons Vann's green tea rub
> ¼ cup finely chopped scallions, white and light green parts only
> 4 medium lobsters, poached, cooled, and split in half
> 8 thin slices of lemon, for garnish

1. Combine the mayonnaise and green tea rub in a small bowl. Let it stand for 1 hour at room temperature, or covered in the refrigerator for several hours. Before serving, stir the scallions into the mayonnaise.
2. Place a lobster half on each of the 8 plates. Spoon a generous dollop of the mayonnaise over each lobster, add a lemon slice, and serve.

Broiled Bluefish with Green Tea Salt

Serves 4

Green tea mixed with coarse salt sprinkled over broiled fish adds a subtle, smoky flavor, says Mark Bittman, who writes "The Minimalist" column in the *New York Times*. Green tea's delicate taste, especially when combined with lemon or lime, cuts through full-flavored fish and adds a special dimension. As a variation, broil red snapper or swordfish, brushed on both sides with one to two tablespoons melted butter. For thicker steaks, cook for about ten minutes and turn once. Use a lemon instead of a lime.

> 1½ to 2 pounds bluefish, mackerel, or halibut fillets
> 1 tablespoon toasted sesame oil
> 1 tablespoon finely ground green tea
> 1½ teaspoons coarse salt
> 1 lime, cut into quarters

1. Preheat the broiler and position the rack as close to the heating element as possible, as close as 2 inches away. Arrange the fish on the broiling pan, skin side down, and brush lightly with sesame oil.
2. Broil the fish, checking once or twice to make sure it is browning but not burning; lower the rack if necessary. When the fish is browned and a thin-bladed knife penetrates the flesh with little resistance, it is done, about 5 minutes in a good broiler.
3. Combine the tea and salt and sprinkle liberally over the fish. Serve with lime wedges.

Recipe courtesy of Mark Bittman

Poached scallops with red peppers and vanilla tea vinaigrette.

Poached Scallops with Red Peppers and Vanilla Tea Vinaigrette

Serves 2 to 3

Sweet shellfish—including lobster and scallops—are willing partners for vanilla's tropical fragrance. Here plump sea scallops are gently simmered in vanilla-scented tea. The poaching liquor is then reduced to a couple of tablespoons and becomes part of a sweet-tangy warm vinaigrette. Serve over jasmine rice.

1 tablespoon vanilla H_T tea leaves
1 pound sea scallops, tough, opaque parts removed
1 small clove garlic
1 tablespoon honey
1 tablespoon balsamic vinegar
¼ cup extra-virgin olive oil
Salt and freshly ground black pepper
1 large red bell pepper, cut into small dice
2 to 3 tablespoons coarsely chopped cilantro leaves or chives

1. Bring 1 cup of water just to a boil, pour over the tea, and infuse for 5 minutes. Strain into a large skillet, pressing to extract as much liquid as possible. Bring the tea to a simmer, add the scallops, and cook just until opaque, about 4 minutes. Remove the scallops with a slotted spoon to a bowl and reduce the liquid over high heat to 3 tablespoons. Combine with the garlic, honey, vinegar, and olive oil in an electric blender and blend until emulsified. Season to taste with salt and pepper. Pour over the scallops and, if desired, let them marinate a couple of hours or overnight covered in the refrigerator to intensify the marinade flavor.

2. When ready to serve, return the scallops to the skillet and add the diced pepper. Turn the heat to medium-high, pour on the vinaigrette, and shake the pan to quickly heat the scallops through. Sprinkle with cilantro and serve.

Earl Grey–Crusted Salmon

Serves 4

Aside from being delicious, salmon is now so reasonably priced, readily available, and healthful we all need a variety of ways to prepare it. With a warm-spice coating of tea scented with bergamot, played against juniper berries, mace, and orange zest, and baked with orange slices, this fish will never be mundane.

> 1 orange
> 12 juniper berries
> 2 tablespoons Earl Grey or other black tea leaves
> ½ teaspoon black peppercorns
> ½ teaspoon ground mace
> ½ teaspoon salt
> 2 teaspoons unsalted butter
> 1½ to 2 pounds center-cut salmon fillets, skin left on,
>   cut into 4 pieces and patted dry
> Salt and freshly ground black pepper
> 1 tablespoon finely chopped flat-leaf parsley, for garnish

1. Preheat the oven to 350° F.
2. Grate the orange zest and reserve. Pare off the pith from the orange, slice it crosswise, and set aside. Combine the zest with the juniper berries, tea leaves, peppercorns, mace, and salt in a spice or coffee grinder and grind into a powder. It will be somewhat moist.
3. Melt the butter in a large, oven-safe heavy skillet over medium-high heat. Season the salmon with salt and pepper to taste. Sauté it, flesh side down, until brown, about 5 minutes. Turn with a spatula, sprinkle on the tea-spice mixture, and spoon any butter over the fish. Place the orange slices on the fish.
4. Bake until the salmon is just cooked through, about 8 to 10 minutes. If desired, briefly run the skillet under the broiler to brown the oranges a little. Remove, sprinkle with the parsley, and serve.

Earl Grey of Howick Hall, Northumberland, was one of Britain's most popular prime ministers. His 1832 Reform Act completely changed the democratic system in Britain to today's parliamentary constituencies of roughly equal size and a one man, one vote electoral system. As prime minister, he sent a diplomatic mission to China and, by chance, the envoy saved the life of a Chinese Mandarin. In gratitude, the Mandarin sent the Earl an exquisitely scented tea along with its recipe. The special ingredient with which it was flavored was oil of bergamot. Earl Grey was delighted and in the future always asked his tea merchant—the Tyneside company, Twinings—for it. His drawing room soon became famous for its tea and, in due course, the family gave permission for the blend to be sold to the public. Today, Earl Grey is the world's most popular blend and is sold in more than 90 countries.

From *The Secret Kingdom*, North Northumberland, England

Black and white sesame–crusted sole.

Black and White Sesame–Crusted Sole

Serves 2

Oolong tea in the crunchy coating of these sole fillets subtly complements the nutty taste of sesame seeds. Black and white seeds—although they taste alike—make the coating visually more appealing, as does the final sprinkle of scallions.

> ⅓ cup *each* black and white sesame seeds or ⅔ cup either one
> 2 tablespoons oolong tea leaves, finely ground
> ¾ pound sole, flounder, or similar white fish fillets, blotted dry
> 2 to 3 tablespoons sesame oil
> Salt and freshly ground black pepper
> Thinly sliced scallion, including green part, for garnish

1. Blend the sesame seeds and tea together in a flat dish. Brush the fillets generously with some of the sesame oil. Season both sides with salt and pepper to taste and press the fillets into the sesame mixture so the seeds stick to the fish.

2. Heat the remaining oil in a large nonstick skillet over medium-high heat until hot. Cook the fish for about 2 minutes, or until the seeds are light brown, adding a little more oil if the pan is dry. Carefully slide a spatula under the fillets and turn, cooking the second side until the seeds are golden brown and the fish is just cooked through, about 2 minutes more. Remove, sprinkle with scallions, and serve immediately.

Harney's Cinnamon Spice Tea –
Smoked Swordfish Steaks

Serves 6

Traditional Chinese tea smoking uses black tea. Chef Danny Lee, who has known the Harneys and their teas for decades, uses their Hot Cinnamon Spice ^H_T tea leaves to impart a mystical, smoky flavor to swordfish. ⌗ Experiment with different teas and/or combinations of teas to enhance smoked foods, as you would with different varieties of woods.

> **2 ounces peanut shells**
> **2 tablespoons Hot Cinnamon Spice ^H_T or other spice-scented**
> **blends of tea leaves**
> **2 tablespoons dark brown sugar**
> **Six 8-ounce slices center-cut swordfish steaks**
> **Salt and freshly ground black pepper**

1. Line a wok, pot, or deep roasting pan with 2 to 3 layers of heavy-duty aluminum foil. Combine the peanut shells with the tea leaves and brown sugar and sprinkle in the prepared pan. Set a Chinese smoking net or rack on top.

2. Lightly season the swordfish with salt and pepper, then place it on the netting. Wrap the foil over the top of the pan, tightly, crimping it, place it over high heat, and smoke for 3 minutes. Carefully open the pan and serve the fish.

Seared Tuna and Fennel over Jasmine Rice

Serves 4

Jasmine rice's fragrant aroma blossoms into a lush bouquet of taste when the rice is cooked in jasmine tea. The perfumed rice is a perfect partner to seared rare tuna slices and fennel wedges simmered in coconut milk and Pernod. Jasmine tea derives its floral essence from fresh jasmine flowers layered into the tea. Many teas can be used to add flavor to rice. Try fruit and spice teas, such as Peach & Ginger [H][T] for summer rice salads and black currant or Cranberry Autumn Blend [H][T] for wild rice dishes.

1¾ to 2 cups water, according to directions on rice package
2 teaspoons jasmine tea leaves
1 cup jasmine or long-grain white rice
1 teaspoon salt, or as needed
4 tablespoons extra-virgin olive oil
1 medium onion, cut into medium dice
4 ounces button mushrooms, wiped, trimmed, and sliced
1 large bulb fennel, trimmed, reserving fronds, cored, and
   cut top to bottom into thin wedges
4 tuna steaks, about 6 to 8 ounces each, cut 1¼ inch thick, and patted dry
Salt and freshly ground black pepper
⅓ cup Pernod or other anise-flavored liqueur
½ cup coconut milk

1. Bring the water just to a boil, add the tea leaves, remove from the heat, and infuse for 3 to 4 minutes. Strain, discard the tea leaves, and combine the liquid with the rice and 1 teaspoon salt in a heavy saucepan. Bring the liquid to a boil, tightly cover the pan, reduce the heat, and simmer until the rice is tender and all the liquid has been absorbed, about 20 minutes.
2. Meanwhile, heat 2 tablespoons of the olive oil in a large skillet over medium-high heat. Add the onion and sauté until wilted and lightly golden, about 5 minutes. Stir in the mushrooms and continue cooking, stirring frequently, until just softened, about 2 minutes more. Once the rice is cooked, stir in the onions and mushrooms and keep warm.
3. Heat 1 tablespoon of the remaining olive oil in the large skillet over medium-high heat. Add the fennel wedges and sauté until the edges begin to brown and the fennel is crisp-tender, about 4 to 5 minutes. Remove the fennel to a plate.
4. Brush the tuna with a little of the remaining olive oil and season to taste with salt and pepper. Heat the

skillet until very hot over high heat. Add the tuna steaks and cook until rare or medium-rare, according to taste, about 1½ to 2½ minutes per side, turning once. Remove to a warm plate and tent lightly to keep warm.

5. Turn off the heat. Carefully pour the Pernod into the skillet and ignite away from your face. Once the flames subside, pour in the coconut milk and bring the liquid to a boil, stirring to incorporate any browned cooking bits. Return the fennel to the pan, turning to coat with the sauce. Adjust the salt and pepper to taste.

6. To serve, spoon a generous mound of rice onto each of 4 warmed plates. Cut the tuna steaks across the grain into ½-inch slices, and lay on the rice. Spoon the fennel and sauce over the tuna and rice. Garnish each plate with a small fennel frond and serve.

Whole Tea-Smoked Chicken

Serves 4 to 6

Grace Young, a talented Chinese cookbook author, most recently of the award-winning *Wisdom of the Chinese Kitchen*, describes this traditional north and western Chinese style steam-smoked chicken as magnificently aromatic and looking like burnished mahogany. For perfect results, don't rush the preparation; allow two days.

Tea smoking can produce a lot of smoke. It shows the process is working. Don't walk away from the stove, though, as you need to watch the process carefully. Also, throw the smoking mixture away immediately after use to prevent the odor from permeating your home.

10 cups plus 3 cups water
3 tablespoons soy sauce
½ cup rice wine, available at Asian markets and most supermarkets
2 tablespoons salt
1 tablespoon sesame oil
2 tablespoons Szechuan peppercorns
1-inch piece fresh ginger
2 cinnamon sticks
3 star anise
One 3½-pound chicken, excess fat removed, rinsed
1 cup black tea leaves
1 cup long-grain rice
½ cup (firmly packed) light or dark brown sugar
4 pieces dried orange peel

1. Combine 10 cups of water, the soy sauce, rice wine, salt, sesame oil, 1 tablespoon Szechuan peppercorns, the ginger, 1 cinnamon stick, and 1 star anise in a large pot. Bring to a boil over medium-high heat. Reduce the heat to low and simmer, uncovered, for 10 minutes. Let the liquid cool completely. Add the chicken, breast side down, and cover. Refrigerate for 24 hours.
2. Transfer the chicken from the liquid to a shallow heatproof bowl that will fit inside a bamboo steamer. Place the bowl inside and cover the steamer with a lid. Bring 3 cups of water to a boil in a wok. Place

the covered steamer in the wok and steam the chicken for 45 minutes, or about 15 minutes per pound, checking the water level and replenishing as needed.

3. Oil a metal rack. Turn off the heat and carefully remove the chicken from the steamer. Place it on the rack. Drain the liquid in the cavity and combine it with any accumulated liquid in the bowl used for steaming. Reserve for serving.

4. Combine the tea, rice, brown sugar, the remaining 1 tablespoon peppercorns, orange peel, the remaining cinnamon stick, and the remaining 2 star anise in a large bowl. Line a 14-inch wok with 2 to 3 layers of heavy-duty aluminum foil, leaving a 3- to 4-inch overhang. Pour the tea mixture into the wok and set the chicken on the rack over it. The chicken should rest 2 inches above the tea mixture. Turn on the exhaust fan on the stove or open the windows to create cross ventilation.

5. Turn the heat to high. The chicken will start smoking in 3 to 4 minutes. Cover the wok with the lid, crimp the foil overhang tightly against the lid, and smoke for 10 minutes. If the smoke is escaping, crimp the foil more tightly. Let the wok rest for 5 minutes, then carefully remove the lid, away from your face. If the chicken is light brown, smoke it for 10 minutes more. If it is already dark, smoke it for 5 minutes more.

6. Reheat the smoking materials: Heat the wok, uncovered, until there is smoke, about 3 to 4 minutes. Re-cover the chicken, crimp the foil, and smoke until the chicken is the color of mahogany. Turn off the heat and let the chicken rest for 10 minutes.

7. Carefully remove the lid, transfer the chicken to a platter. Once the smoking mixture is cool enough to handle, wrap it in the foil and throw it away. Cut the chicken into serving pieces and serve warm or at room temperature with the reserved cooking liquid.

Adapted from Grace Young's recipe in *The Best of China*.

Baked Indian Chicken Breasts

Serves 4

In India, traditional clay ovens called "tandoors" are used to cook foods that have been marinated in yogurt and spices over very high temperature. The results are sublimely perfumed and juicy meats, poultry, and fish. An Indian spiced tea and yogurt marinade similarly tenderizes chicken breasts and adds extraordinary flavor to the meat.

1 small onion, chopped
1 large clove garlic
2 tablespoons fresh lemon juice
1 tablespoon Indian Spice^H_T or other cinnamon spice–scented
    tea leaves, finely ground
2 teaspoons paprika
½ cup plain yogurt, regular or low-fat
1 teaspoon salt or as needed
Freshly ground black pepper to taste
4 large boneless chicken breasts, skin on, with as much fat removed as possible
1 tablespoon unsalted butter
Several sprigs of watercress, for garnish
Lemon wedges, for garnish

1. Combine the onion, garlic, lemon juice, tea, paprika, yogurt, 1 teaspoon salt, and pepper to taste in an electric blender and purée until smooth. Scrape the mixture into a large, resealable plastic bag, and add the chicken breasts, turning to coat evenly. Seal and refrigerate overnight or for at least 8 hours, turning once or twice.
2. Preheat the oven to 350°F.
3. Remove the breasts from the plastic bag, scraping off the marinade. Reserve the marinade. Season the breasts with salt and pepper to taste. Melt the butter in a nonstick skillet large enough to hold them in 1 layer over medium-high heat. Add the breasts, skin side down, and cook until rich golden brown. Turn, scrape the reserved yogurt mixture over the breasts, and transfer the pan to the oven.
4. Bake until the breasts are just cooked through, 35 to 45 minutes depending on their size. Remove to a warm platter. Reduce the remaining yogurt in the pan over high heat until thick enough to pour over the breasts. Garnish with watercress and lemon and serve.

Peach and ginger–glazed chicken legs with crisp yuca wedges (page 80).

Peach and Ginger–Glazed Chicken Legs

Serves 4

This Asian-inspired glaze brushed over chicken legs and thighs (or breasts, if you prefer) turns them into a juicy main course with a minimum of fuss. If you prefer, you can skin the legs before cooking. Make a large quantity of the glaze and store it in the refrigerator to brush over salmon or shrimp as well as chicken.

⅔ **cup peach preserves**
2 **tablespoons chopped fresh ginger**
2 **cloves garlic**
2 **tablespoons soy sauce**
1 **tablespoon English Breakfast or other black tea leaves**
Crushed red pepper (optional)
4 **chicken legs with thighs, preferably of equal size, blotted dry**
1 **to 2 teaspoons vegetable oil**
Salt and freshly ground black pepper
1 **to 2 tablespoons chopped cilantro or flat-leaf parsley, for garnish**

1. Preheat the oven to 350° F.
2. Purée the preserves, ginger, garlic, soy sauce, and tea leaves in an electric blender until smooth and scrape down the sides. If desired, add the red pepper to taste. Set aside.
3. Lightly brush the chicken legs with oil. Heat a large, heavy, ovensafe skillet over medium-high heat. Put the legs, skin side down, in the pan and brown well, 6 to 8 minutes. Season to taste with salt and pepper, turn, season the second side with salt and pepper, and pour on the glaze.
4. Transfer the pan to the oven and bake until the chicken is cooked through and the glaze has thickened, about 40 minutes, spooning the glaze over the legs once or twice. Remove the pan from the oven, sprinkle with a little cilantro, and serve.

Breast of Duck with Curried Dried Fruit Chutney

Serves 4

Few condiments are as simple and tasty as this chutney: Simply pour strong mint tea over dried fruit. Stir in some Indian curry paste (your choice of mild or hot) and let the fruit absorb the flavors. You'll savor the subtle mint taste at the back of your palate. Also serve the chutney with roast chicken, full-flavored grilled fish, or even a grilled cheese sandwich. Duck breasts, available at many butchers and specialty stores, allow the pleasure of eating the best part of the bird without the fuss and time needed to cook duck whole. Serve the breasts medium-rare to savor the duck's juicy flavor.

Minted Curried Fruit Chutney

2 tablespoons Moroccan Mint ^H_T tea leaves

1½ cups mixed dried fruits, such as cranberries, apricots, cherries, prunes, and dates

1 to 2 tablespoons mild Indian curry paste

Duck Breasts

2 whole boneless Peking duck breasts, excess fat removed, skin and fat scored diagonally into small squares

Salt and freshly ground black pepper

Fresh mint leaves, for garnish

1. To prepare the chutney, bring 2 cups of water just to a boil. Pour it over the tea and steep for 3 minutes. Strain, pressing to extract as much liquid as possible. Combine the dried fruits in a saucepan. Stir the curry paste into the tea and pour it over the fruit. Bring the mixture to a boil, turn off heat, cover the pan, and allow the fruit to soften, at least 20 to 30 minutes, adding more hot water as needed to soften the fruit.

2. To cook the duck, season both sides of the duck breasts with salt and pepper to taste. Heat a large heavy skillet over medium-high heat until very hot. Lay the duck breasts in the pan, skin side down, without any butter or fat. Cook until all the fat has been rendered from beneath the skin, about 8 minutes, checking to avoid burning. Discard the fat as it accumulates. Flip the breasts over and lower the heat to medium-low. Spoon some of the chutney over the breasts, partially cover the pan, and cook until the breasts are medium-rare, about 6 minutes more.

3. Cut the breasts in half, then, if desired, across the grain into 1/2-inch slices. Add a few mint leaves and serve. Pass the extra chutney at the table.

Szechuan Tea–Smoked Duck

Serves 4 to 6

Tea-smoked duck is a Szechuan Chinese dish. In this version, Chef Danny Lee, associate professor of culinary arts at the Culinary Institute of America and a great friend of the Harney family, makes a succulent, mahogany lacquered bird without a smoker. You can cook the duck right after it's seasoned, but refrigerating the unseasoned bird, uncovered, on a rack (over a plate or pan) for a day tightens the skin, helping to keep the meat juicy and the skin crisp. Serve this duck hot or at room temperature. The skin coloring mixture can be refrigerated for months. ✿ For best results when smoking a large bird, cook it first and smoke it afterwards. To prevent seafood from drying out, smoke it first and then cook it until done.

One 5-pound Peking duck, rinsed and blotted dry

Skin Seasoning Mixture

¼ cup coarse salt
1 teaspoon garlic powder
1 teaspoon ground white pepper

Skin Coloring Mixture

6 tablespoons light soy sauce
2 teaspoons rice wine or sherry (available at many liquor stores
    and Asian markets)
1 tablespoon yellow food coloring
½ teaspoon red food coloring

Cavity Seasoning Mixture

6 scallions, roughly chopped, including green parts
6 cloves garlic, coarsely chopped
3 ounces fresh ginger, coarsely chopped
3 star anise, broken into pieces
2 tablespoons Szechuan peppercorns
¼ cup coarse salt
1 tablespoon freshly ground black pepper

Smoking

2 ounces peanut shells

2 tablespoons jasmine tea leaves
2 tablespoons sugar
Chopped cilantro or scallions, for garnish

1. Cut off the first 2 wing joints from the duck and reserve. Make a small incision between the remaining drummettes and the body of the duck. Remove excess fat and the tail and trim the neck skin to about 2 inches from the shoulders.
2. To make the skin seasoning mixture, combine the salt with the garlic powder and white pepper. Rub the seasoning mixture over the duck's skin.
3. To make the skin coloring mixture, combine the soy sauce, rice wine, and food colorings in a small bowl. Brush the skin and inside of the neck cavity lightly and evenly with the mixture.
4. To make the cavity seasoning mixture, mix the scallions, garlic, ginger, star anise, Szechuan peppercorns, salt, and black pepper together. Season inside the duck with the mixture. Place the reserved wing tips on a wire rack and place the duck on top of them to prevent the duck from sticking to the rack. Set in a roasting pan or on a sheet pan and refrigerate overnight.
5. Preheat the oven to 350°F.
6. Roast the duck, uncovered, on the rack for 1½ hours, or until the juices run clear when the duck is pierced deep in the thigh joint. Remove from the oven.
7. Meanwhile, for smoking, cover the bottom of a wok, pot, or deep roasting pan with 2 to 3 large pieces of heavy-duty aluminum foil, then sprinkle on the peanut shells, tea, and sugar. Set a rack that fits inside the pan or a Chinese smoking net over the smoking materials.
8. Transfer the duck to the rack or smoking net and cover the pan tightly, crimping the foil close to the wok. Place the pan over high heat for 3 minutes if using a wok, or for up to 8 minutes in a roasting pan or pot. The duck should be dark rich golden brown with crispy, shiny skin.
9. Carefully take off the lid. Remove the duck, cut it into pieces 1 inch wide by 2 inches long, and transfer it to a serving platter. Serve hot or at room temperature, garnished with cilantro or scallions.

Szechuan tea–smoked duck.

Tea-Smoked Quail over Spinach

Serves 6 as a first course

Quail are small enough to tea-smoke without precooking. Serve them no more done than medium, the ideal degree of doneness for these juicy, little birds.

6 quail
1½ tablespoons Szechuan peppercorns
2 tablespoons coarse salt
1 scallion, including green part, chopped
1-inch piece fresh ginger
1 clove garlic
⅓ Lapsang souchong tea leaves
⅓ cup raw rice
¼ cup (firmly packed) dark or light brown sugar
1 tablespoon Chinese five-spice powder
1 strip of orange zest, about 3 inches long, coarsely chopped
2 tablespoons Asian sesame oil, available at Asian markets and
    most supermarkets
8 ounces spinach leaves, rinsed with a little water left on the leaves
Rice vinegar
Salt and freshly ground black pepper
1 tablespoon black sesame seeds, lightly toasted
Sliced scallions for garnish

1. Remove the necks, feet, and innards from the quail and discard. Cut off the first 2 wing joints of each bird and reserve. Rinse the quail and blot dry. Combine the Szechuan peppercorns, salt, scallion, ginger, and garlic in a blender and purée into a smooth paste. Rub the mixture over the quail, including the insides. Set the birds on a rack and refrigerate for 2 to 3 hours.
2. Cover the bottom of a wok, pot, or deep roasting pan with 2 to 3 pieces of heavy-duty aluminum foil. Toss the tea, rice, sugar, five-spice powder, and orange zest together and sprinkle on the foil. Place a rack that fits inside the pan and stands about 2 inches above the smoking materials on top and put the reserved wing tips on it.

3. Lay the quail, breast side up, on the wing tips and cover the pan, leaving a small space for steam to escape. Place the pan over high heat and smoke for about 8 minutes, or until the birds are rich brown with the flesh medium-rare. If you would like them more well-done, place them in a 400°F oven for 4 to 8 minutes, to taste. Remove the pan from the heat and let stand for 5 minutes. Carefully uncover.

4. Meanwhile, heat a large skillet until hot. Add the oil and spinach leaves and sauté until just wilted. Season the spinach with rice vinegar, salt, and pepper to taste, and toss with the sesame seeds. Divide the spinach among 6 salad plates. Cut each quail in half and lay it on the spinach. Sprinkle with scallions and serve.

Tastea Turkey Meat Loaf

Serves 4

So the name's a little corny, but this turkey meat loaf—perfumed with smoky Lapsang souchong tea and Thai sweet chili sauce—really does afford a big hit of taste without a lot of calories. Plus, it's nice and juicy. (If you don't like smoky tastes, use any black tea.) You can easily make this in a food processor, but just pulse the motor as you mix the ingredients to keep the mixture light.

>   2 tablespoons olive oil
>   1½ cups finely chopped onions
>   2 large cloves garlic
>   1 medium carrot, coarsely chopped
>   ½ red bell pepper, seeded and membranes removed, coarsely chopped
>   ¼ cup chopped cilantro
>   1¼ pounds ground turkey
>   1 tablespoon Lapsang souchong tea leaves, finely ground
>   1 egg, lightly beaten
>   ½ cup fresh bread crumbs
>   3 tablespoons sweet Thai chili sauce, available at Thai markets and
>   some supermarkets
>   1 teaspoon salt, or as needed
>   Freshly ground black pepper

1. Preheat the oven to 350°F.
2. Heat the oil in a large skillet over medium-high heat. Add the onions and sauté until wilted and lightly browned, about 5 to 6 minutes. Set aside.
3. Pulse the garlic, carrot, and bell pepper in a food processor until minced. Add the cilantro, pulse to blend, then put in the turkey, tea, egg, bread crumbs, 2 tablespoons of the Thai chili sauce, salt, and pepper to taste. Pulse just until blended. Do not overmix. Transfer the mixture to a 9 x 5-inch loaf pan, patting lightly until smooth. Spread the remaining tablespoon of Thai chili sauce over the top.
4. Bake for 45 minutes, or until the juices run clear. Remove and let stand 5 to 10 minutes, then cut into slices and serve. Or serve at room temperature.

Spicy-Smoky Baked Spareribs

Serves 4

There are lots of fancy barbecue sauces on the market, many with high price tags. With just a little imagination, some canned, smoked Jalapeño peppers, and a bit of tea, you can turn the most mundane sauce into sophisticated, smoky-spicy ribs that taste like a million bucks. You're sure to like these meaty, fork-tender ribs. The sauce ingredients and amount of ribs can easily be doubled to feed more people. And you can experiment with different teas.

> **3½ to 4 pounds pork or beef spareribs**
> **Salt and freshly ground black pepper to taste**
> **2 cups tomato-based barbecue sauce**
> **¼ cup gunpowder or Lapsang souchong tea leaves, finely ground**
> **2 to 3 teaspoons canned chipotle chile sauce, or as needed**

1. Preheat the oven to 400°F. Line a large, shallow baking pan with heavy-duty aluminum foil.
2. Season the ribs with salt and pepper, place on the foil, flesh side down, and put in the oven. Immediately adjust the heat to 300°F. Bake for 30 minutes.
3. Blend the barbecue sauce with the tea leaves and chipotle chile sauce. After 30 minutes, remove the ribs from oven, drain off any accumulated fat, and turn the ribs over. Brush the sauce on the ribs, return to the oven, and bake until fork-tender, about 1 to 1½ hours. Remove, let stand at least 5 minutes, and serve.

Sauteed pork chops with apricot–wild mushroom glaze with coconut-scented yams (page 73).

Sautéed Pork Chops with Apricot–Wild Mushroom Glaze

Serves 4

These pork chops are easy yet so enticing, you can treat yourself to a festive dinner any night of the week. Brewed Lapsang souchong tea is absorbed into the dried mushrooms, imparting a smoky-winey taste that complements the sweet apricot preserves.

½ **cup water**
2 **teaspoons Lapsang souchong tea leaves**
½ **ounce mixed dried wild mushrooms**
½ **cup apricot preserves**
1 **teaspoon unsalted butter or canola oil**
4 **rib pork chops, about 1-inch thick, blotted dry**
Salt and freshly ground black pepper to taste
¼ **cup dry white wine**
Chopped flat-leaf parsley, for garnish

1. Bring the water just to a boil, pour over the tea, and infuse for 5 minutes. Strain the tea over the wild mushrooms, pressing to extract as much liquid as possible. Allow the mushrooms to soften, about 15 minutes. Do not drain. Combine the softened mushrooms and any remaining liquid with the apricot preserves, stirring to blend well.
2. Heat the butter or oil over medium-high heat in a skillet just large enough to hold the pork chops. Cook until browned on one side, about 5 minutes. Generously season with salt and pepper, turn, and season the second side. Pour the preserve mixture over the meat, and adjust the heat to medium-low. Cover and cook until the pork is barely pink in the center, about 8 minutes.
3. Remove the chops to a heated platter, pour the wine into the skillet, bring the liquid to a boil, and stir up any browned cooking bits. Pour the sauce over the chops, sprinkle on parsley, and serve.

Seared Steak with Tea'd Pan Sauce

Serves 2

In no more time than it takes to cook a New York steak to medium-rare, you can make this distinctive pan sauce to serve on top of it. Use almost any tea of your choice. Instead of deglazing the pan with wine, tea and rice wine vinegar followed by a dash of balsamic vinegar will do the job.

> 2 tablespoons Irish Breakfast, Earl Grey, or other black tea leaves
> 1 teaspoon vegetable oil
> 1 New York shell steak, about 1 to 1¼ inches thick, well trimmed
>   and blotted dry
> Salt and freshly ground black pepper
> ¼ cup finely chopped shallots
> 1 tablespoon rice wine vinegar
> 5 tablespoons unsalted butter, cut into pieces, at room temperature
> Balsamic vinegar
> 2 teaspoons minced flat-leaf parsley

1. Bring 1 cup of water just to a boil, pour it over the tea and steep for 5 minutes. Strain, pressing to extract as much liquid as possible, and set aside.
2. Preheat the oven to 400°F. Place an ovensafe pan inside to heat.
3. Heat a medium-size skillet over medium-high heat until hot. Add the oil, then the steak, and cook until richly browned on 1 side, 4 to 5 minutes. Season to taste with salt and pepper, turn, and cook the second side until browned, about 4 minutes. Season with salt and pepper, then transfer the steak to the pan in the the oven. Turn oven down to warm.
4. Add the shallots to the skillet, lower the heat to medium, and cook until limp and lightly browned, 2 to 3 minutes, stirring often. Pour in the rice vinegar and tea, turn the heat to high, and boil until the liquid is reduced by about two thirds, scraping up all the browned cooking bits.
5. Turn the heat to low. Whisk in the butter, a piece at a time, until all the butter is incorporated. Season to taste with pepper, salt, and balsamic vinegar.
6. Remove the steak from the oven. Drain any pan juices into the sauce and cut the meat across the grain into 1/2-inch slices. Divide it between 2 plates, spoon on the sauce, sprinkle with the parsley, and serve.

Slowly Braised Lamb Shanks

Serves 2

Time-Enz Harvest, in Salisbury, Connecticut, draws many locals and visitors to its cheery old-fashioned take-out and eat-in spot. Slowly-braised lamb shanks are one of chef-partner Robert Timans's most celebrated dishes. In this exotic version he perfumes the sauce with Moroccan Mint $^H{}_T$ tea leaves. Serve the shanks over basmati rice and drizzle with plain yogurt and mint leaves to garnish.

1 quart orange juice
½ cup Moroccan Mint $^H{}_T$ tea leaves
Two 1½-pound lamb shanks, blotted dry
Salt and freshly ground black pepper
1 cup dry mustard
1 teaspoon ground cumin seeds
1 teaspoon ground coriander seeds
½ teaspoon Hungarian sweet paprika
4 tablespoons canola oil
½ cup medium-diced onion
1/2 cup medium-diced carrot

¼ cup medium-diced celery
1 tablespoon chopped garlic
1 tablespoon minced fresh ginger
½ cup tamarind paste
One 32-ounce can crushed tomatoes
2 star anise
1 cinnamon stick
8 peppercorns
Plain yogurt and fresh mint leaves,
    for garnish

1. Bring the orange juice just to a simmer in a nonreactive saucepan. Add the tea leaves and steep for 3 minutes. Strain, pressing to extract as much liquid as possible, and set aside.
2. Season the lamb shanks with salt and pepper. Combine the dry mustard with the cumin, coriander and paprika, and dredge the shanks in the mixture.

3. Heat 2 tablespoons of the oil in a Dutch oven or heavy casserole, and brown the shanks on all sides, then remove and set aside. Wipe out the pot, then heat the remaining oil over medium-high heat. Add the onion, carrot, celery, garlic, and ginger and cook until soft, stirring often.
4. Stir in the tamarind paste. Add the crushed tomatoes, infused orange juice, star anise, cinnamon, and peppercorns. Add the shanks, cover, and slowly simmer until very tender, about 2½ hours, turning occasionally. Remove the shanks, bring the sauce to a boil and reduce it to the desired consistency. Top with the shanks, ladle on the sauce, drizzle with yogurt and sprinkle with mint leaves, and serve.

A woman is like a tea bag—you can't tell how strong she is
until you put her in hot water.

Nancy Reagan

Vegetables and Side Dishes

Glazed Acorn Squash
Curried Potatoes, Cauliflower, and Mushrooms
Coconut-Scented Yams
Japanese Noodle Salad with Sugar Snap Peas
Chamomile Farfalle with Poppy Seeds
Crisp Yuca Wedges
Southwestern Grits
Savory Bread Pudding
Succotash Polenta

Glazed acorn squash.

Glazed Acorn Squash

Serves 2

With the simple addition of spicy cinnamon tea to an orange juice—honey glaze, along with a final shower of chopped pecans, this hearty winter vegetable takes on new style. You could also use Harney's Indian Spice ^H_T tea, Passion Plum ^H_T tea, or any other spiced tea for the glaze.

1 acorn squash, cut in half lengthwise, seeds and membranes removed
½ cup orange juice
2 tablespoons Hot Cinnamon Spice ^H_T or other cinnamon-spice blend tea leaves
2 tablespoons honey
½ teaspoon salt, or as needed
2 teaspoons unsalted butter
1 tablespoon chopped pecans

1. Preheat the oven to 375°F. Lightly brush a baking sheet with oil.
2. Place the squash halves, cut side down, on the baking sheet. Bake until the squash is tender when pushed with a finger, about 50 to 60 minutes.
3. Meanwhile, bring the orange juice just to a simmer in a small saucepan. Stir in the tea leaves and infuse for 5 minutes. Strain, pressing to extract as much liquid as possible. Rinse out the saucepan. Return the tea-infused orange juice to the pan, add the honey and salt, and bring to a boil. Cook until the glaze has thickened and reduced to about 2 tablespoons, about 3 minutes. Stir in the butter and set aside.
4. Once the squash is tender, turn it over, spoon on all of the glaze, sprinkle with pecans, and run it under the broiler until the nuts and glaze are lightly browned, watching that they don't burn. Remove and serve.

Curried Potatoes, Cauliflower, and Mushrooms

Serves 6

Inspired by an Indian vegetarian dish, this combination of potatoes, cauliflower, and mushrooms, simmered with smoky tea–scented yogurt and curry paste, is a flavorful side dish to serve warm or at room temperature.

> 1 pound small Yukon Gold or red-skinned potatoes, scrubbed
> 1 pound cauliflower florets (1 small head cauliflower), broken into small pieces
> ¼ cup water
> 2 tablespoons Lapsang souchong tea leaves
> ½ cup plain yogurt
> 2 tablespoons mild Indian curry paste
> 2 teaspoons cornstarch dissolved in 2 tablespoons water
> 2 tablespoons unsalted butter or canola oil
> 1 medium onion, diced
> 8 ounces small button mushrooms, trimmed and sliced
> Salt and freshly ground black pepper
> 1 to 2 tablespoons finely chopped fresh tarragon leaves

1. In a medium saucepan, boil the potatoes in salted water until tender. Drain and when cool enough to handle, cut them into quarters. Meanwhile, in another saucepan, boil the cauliflower in salted water until tender, then drain. Wipe out the saucepan.
2. Bring 1/4 cup of water just to a boil, pour it over the tea, steep for 5 minutes. Strain, pressing to extract as much liquid as possible. Blend the tea with the yogurt, curry paste, and cornstarch.
3. Heat the butter in the saucepan over medium-high heat. When hot, add the onions and sauté until wilted and beginning to brown. Stir in the mushrooms and cook until they begin to wilt.
4. Scrape the yogurt mixture into the pan, stirring up all the browned cooking bits. Add the potatoes and cauliflower to the pan and stir over medium-high heat until the yogurt is slightly thickened. Season to taste with salt and pepper, add the tarragon, stir again, and serve.

Coconut-Scented Yams

Serves 4 to 6

My son Ben came up with this tempting dish. Roasting yams allows the natural sugars to caramelize, making them sweeter. Rose hips tea or any other kind of tea—including ginger, green, or Lapsang souchong—infused in coconut milk is exceptional. You can make these yams ahead and reheat them.

4 medium yams
1 cup coconut milk
2 tablespoons rose hips tea leaves
Salt
Toasted shredded coconut, for garnish (optional)

1. Preheat the oven to 400° F.
2. Bake the yams until completely tender.
3. Meanwhile bring the coconut milk to a simmer in a saucepan. Stir in the tea and infuse for 5 minutes. Strain, pressing to extract as much liquid as possible.
4. Mash the yams, stir in the tea-infused coconut milk, and season to taste with salt. Garnish with coconut, if desired, and serve.

Japanese noodle salad with sugar snap peas.

Japanese Noodle Salad with Sugar Snap Peas

Serves 6 as a side dish

Japanese udon noodles simmered in green tea, then tossed with crunchy sugar snap peas, scallions, and black sesame seeds make a colorful and satisfying room-temperature side dish. The noodles are dressed with hoisin sauce thinned with some of the tea. Add tea-smoked chicken or shrimp for a main course salad. Udon noodles have salt in the dough, so taste before adding any additional seasonings.

> **6 cups water**
> **3 tablespoons green tea leaves, such as bancha (see page 6)**
> **8 ounces Japanese udon noodles, available in Asian markets and some supermarkets**
> **1 to 2 tablespoons toasted sesame oil**
> **4 ounces sugar snap peas, strings removed, cooked until crisp-tender**
> **½ cup sliced scallions, including green parts**
> **1 tablespoon black sesame seeds, lightly toasted**
> **2 to 3 tablespoons hoisin sauce**

1. Bring the water almost to a boil, stir in the tea leaves, and steep for 3 minutes. Strain the liquid, pressing to remove as much liquid as possible. Wipe out the pot and return the tea to a boil. Stir in the noodles and cook until just tender but not soggy. Drain the noodles in a colander, reserving some of the tea. Toss the noodles with 1 tablespoon of the sesame oil.

2. Combine the noodles, sugar snap peas, scallions, and sesame seeds in a bowl. Blend 2 tablespoons of the hoisin with 3 tablespoons of the reserved green tea and pour over the noodles. Toss and taste, adding additional oil or hoisin sauce dissolved in tea if needed, and serve. As the noodles sit, they absorb liquid. Add more sauce, as desired.

Chamomile Farfalle with Poppy Seeds

Serves 2

One of my great-grandmother's favorite dishes was bow tie pasta with poppy seeds. It reveals her Austro-Hungarian origins. In this modern interpretation, farfalle (Italian for "butterflies" or "bow ties") are boiled in chamomile tea, adding a lush fragrance to the mild-tasting pasta for this simple side dish. Serve with roast chicken or pot-roasted meats. ✿ Adding a final strong infusion of tea enhances the chamomile flavor without bitterness.

> 4¾ cups water
> 3 chamomile tea bags
> 1 teaspoon salt
> 2 cups uncooked farfalle (bow tie pasta)
> 1 to 2 tablespoons unsalted butter
> 1 teaspoon poppy seeds

1. Bring 4½ cups of the water to a boil, add two of the 3 tea bags, and infuse for 5 minutes. Remove and discard the tea bags. Add the salt, bring to a boil and stir in the pasta. Return the liquid to a boil and cook until the pasta is just al dente, stirring occasionally.
2. While the pasta boils, bring the remaining ¼ cup of water to a boil, add the remaining tea bag, and infuse for 5 minutes. Remove the tea bag and discard. Drain the pasta and return it to the pot. Stir in the butter and the infused ¼ cup chamomile tea and poppy seeds. Cook briefly until the pasta is tender, then serve.

Chamomile farfelle with poppy seeds.

Crisp Yuca Wedges

Serves 4 to 6

The delicate sweet flavor of yuca "fries" is a perfect complement to spicy dishes. Yuca's almost neutral flavor takes well to a light dusting of rooibos tea ground with coarse salt.

Yuca, also known as manioc, tapioca, and cassava, is a starchy root used for everything from appetizers to desserts. Hispanic dishes frequently rely on yuca to thicken dishes, while in the Caribbean, it's often fried.

2 pounds yuca, peeled and cut into 4-inch lengths
Peanut or other vegetable oil, for frying
1 tablespoon rooibos tea leaves (see page 6)
1 tablespoon coarse salt

1. Bring a large pot of salted water to a boil. Add the yuca and cook until a fork easily penetrates the flesh, at least 18 to 20 minutes. Test each piece separately and watch that you don't overcook the yuca. Drain and blot dry, then cut into thick, irregular wedges, like steak fries.
2. Heat ½- to ¾-inch oil in a deep skillet until hot. Add the wedges, a few at a time, and cook over medium-high heat until golden brown, 15 to 20 minutes, turning to color on all sides. Blot on paper towels.
3. Blend the rooibos tea and salt in a smal bwl or grind the tea and salt in a spice grinder until fine and well mixed. Sprinkle over the yuca wedges and serve.

Southwestern Grits

Serves 4 to 6

Grits, a staple of both sophisticated and rustic restaurant menus, are pure comfort food. In our version, green tea adds a subtle herb taste that complements the spicy cheese mixture. Serve the grits with fried eggs for a great Sunday morning brunch treat.

> 1 tablespoon sencha (see page 6) or other green tea leaves
> 1 tablespoon unsalted butter
> 1 teaspoon salt
> ¾ cup quick-cooking grits
> 1½ cups shredded Southwestern-style Jack and/or Cheddar cheeses

1. Bring 3 cups of water just to a boil. Pour it over the tea and infuse for 3 minutes. Strain the tea into a medium-heavy saucepan, pressing to extract as much liquid as possible.
2. Add the butter and salt, and bring to a boil. Whisk in the grits slowly to avoid lumps. Reduce the heat to low and continue cooking until the grits are tender and all the liquid is absorbed, 12 to 15 minutes. Add the cheese and stir until melted. Serve at once.

Savory Bread Pudding

Serves 4 to 6

This sophisticated brunch, lunch, or buffet offering pairs bread soaked in Earl Grey–infused milk with feta cheese and mushrooms. Serve it as a side dish with fish, poultry, or with any kind of grilled sausages for a satisfying main course.

> 1 cup milk
> 3 Earl Grey tea bags or 1 tablespoon Earl Grey tea leaves
> 3 eggs
> 1 teaspoon salt or as needed
> Black pepper
> 4 cups French or Italian bread roughly torn into 1½-inch cubes
> 1½ tablespoons olive oil
> 1 large onion, diced
> 6 ounces button mushrooms, wiped and sliced
> 1 large clove garlic, minced
> 4 ounces feta cheese, crumbled
> 1 tablespoon finely chopped flat-leaf parsley
> ⅓ cup grated imported Parmesan cheese

1. Bring the milk just to a boil, add the tea bags or loose tea, and infuse for 5 minutes. Squeeze the bags or strain the tea, pressing to extract as much liquid as possible, and discard. Beat the eggs and blend with the milk. Season with the salt and pepper to taste. Stir in the bread cubes and let them stand for about 15 minutes to absorb the liquid.
2. Preheat oven to 325° F. Butter an 8-inch square baking dish and set aside.
3. Heat the olive oil in a large skillet over medium-high heat. Sauté the onion and mushrooms until the onions are lightly browned, about 5 minutes, stirring or shaking the pan occasionally. Stir in the garlic and cook 1 minute more.
4. Gently fold the mushroom mixture, feta cheese, and parsley into the bread cubes. Do not overmix. Spoon the pudding into the baking dish.
5. Bake for 40 minutes. Sprinkle with Parmesan cheese and continue baking until the pudding top is puffed and golden brown, about 10 minutes. Remove and let stand for a few minutes before cutting into squares and serving.

Succotash Polenta

Serves 4

"Polenta" is Italian for good old native American cornmeal. Our combination of succotash—from a Penobscot Indian word for a mixture of corn and beans—and cornmeal is a salute to our indigenous ingredients with a modern twist: Adding green tea's earthy scent to the chicken stock enhances the flavor of the cornmeal.

> 3¼ cups chicken stock, or more as needed
> 3 tablespoons green tea leaves, such as bancha (see page 6)
> 1 cup corn, canned shoe peg kernels, drained, or defrosted and cooked frozen kernels
> 1 cup frozen baby lima beans, cooked until tender
> 1 small jalapeño pepper, seeded and minced
> ½ cup light cream or whole milk
> 1 cup quick-cooking polenta
> 1 tablespoon unsalted butter
> 1½ teaspoons chili powder
> Salt and freshly ground black pepper

1. Bring the chicken stock just to a boil. Pour over the tea leaves and steep for 3 minutes. Strain into a medium saucepan, pressing to extract as much liquid as possible.
2. Combine the corn, lima beans, jalapeño, and light cream in a small saucepan and bring to a simmer.
3. Meanwhile, bring the infused stock to a boil. Slowly pour in the polenta, stirring constantly over medium heat until the cornmeal is soft, about 5 minutes. Stir in the corn–lima bean mixture, butter, and chili powder. Season to taste with salt and pepper. The polenta should be soft and creamy. If stiff, add a little more chicken stock or water and heat until hot, then serve.

Another fine thing for the soul, after a meal in the evening, is
one of those herbal teas which French people used to call tisanes. . . .
They smooth out wrinkles in your mind miraculously, and make
you sleep, with sweet dreams, too.

M. F. K. Fisher, *How to Cook a Wolf*

Sweet Breads and Desserts

Candied Ginger and Green Tea Bread
Orange-Cranberry-Jasmine Biscotti
Spiced Plum Gingerbread Cake
Green Fruits in Jasmine Tea Syrup
Broiled Pineapple with Spicy Cinnamon Crème Anglaise Sauce
Baked Peaches with Ricotta and Streusel Topping
Two Queens Rice Pudding
Earl Grey Chocolate Mousse
Jasmine—Tropical Fruit—Coconut Sorbet
Buttermilk—Vanilla Tea Sherbet
Raspberry—Chocolate Mint Tea Frozen Yogurt
Chaice Cream with Blackberry Coulis

Candied Ginger and Green Tea Bread

Makes one 9 x 5-inch loaf

This not-too-sweet tea bread could easily become your newest favorite treat. Enjoy it with jam or au naturel for breakfast. For an afternoon tea snack or as part of a light lunch, top small squares with thin rounds of goat cheese and watercress sprigs or cucumber wafers. When spread with cream cheese and apricot preserves, the bread becomes the ultimate tea sandwich. Powdered green tea leaves give this cake its distinctive color; ginger and lemon add flavorful accents.

Finely ground green tea, called *matcha*, can be purchased for use as part of a ritual Japanese tea ceremony. It is very strong, expensive, and unsuitable for this recipe. A clean coffee mill or spice grinder is all that's needed to pulverize the leaves. You can process the tea in a food processor, but the leaves will not be as finely ground.

> 2 cups all-purpose flour
> 2 teaspoons ground ginger
> 1 teaspoon baking powder
> 1 teaspoon salt
> ¼ teaspoon baking soda
> ¼ cup green tea leaves, such as sencha, finely ground (see page 6)
> ¼ cup finely chopped candied ginger
> Zest of 1 lemon, finely chopped
> 4 eggs
> 1 cup superfine sugar
> ¾ cup mildly fruity virgin olive oil or canola oil
> 2 tablespoons fresh lemon juice
> 2 teaspoons vanilla extract

1. Position a baking rack in the lower third of oven. Preheat the oven to 350° F. Lightly oil a 9 x 5-inch loaf pan. Line with parchment paper.
2. Sift together the flour, ginger, baking powder, salt, and baking soda into a bowl. Stir in the green tea, candied ginger, and lemon zest. Set aside.
3. Break the eggs into a food processor and beat until light in color and frothy, about 1 minute. With the motor running, slowly add the sugar through the feed tube in 3 stages, allowing about 30 seconds between each addition. Combine the oil, lemon juice, and vanilla in a small glass measuring cup and drizzle through the feed tube onto the egg mixture with the motor running.

4. Remove the processor top and add the dry ingredients all at once. Pulse until the mixture is just blended. Scrape the batter into the prepared pan.

5. Bake until a knife inserted in the center comes out clean, 50 to 55 minutes. Remove the pan from the oven and let the cake rest for at least 30 minutes on a rack. When cool, remove cake from pan and wrap tightly in plastic wrap. To serve, slice with a serrated knife.

Candied ginger and green tea bread.

Orange-cranberry-jasmine biscotti.

Orange-Cranberry-Jasmine Biscotti

Makes about 3 dozen

Just as our last tea recipe was about to be typed, Deb Uhlfelder, a gifted cook and friend in Marmaroneck, New York, chimed in with her own contribution: Dried cranberries and oranges set against the delicate floral bouquet of jasmine tea in these perfectly dunkable biscotti. What to serve with them? Jasmine tea, for sure, or a little sherry. Sunsweet packages dried cranberries sweetened with orange juice.

8 tablespoons (1 stick) unsalted butter
¾ cup sugar
2 eggs, lightly beaten
2 tablespoons orange juice
2¼ cups all-purpose flour
2 teaspoons finely ground jasmine tea
1½ teaspoons baking powder
¼ teaspoon salt
¼ cup dried cranberries and oranges (Sunsweet)
½ cup chopped almonds, toasted

1. Preheat the oven to 350° F.
2. Cream the butter and sugar together in a large mixing bowl. Stir in the eggs and orange juice. Sift the flour, tea, baking powder, and salt together, then blend the mixture into the butter. Add the dried cranberries and oranges and the almonds and mix well.
3. Divide the dough in half and shape into 2 flat loaves measuring about 10 X 2 inches. Place the loaves on a cookie sheet about 3 inches apart. Bake until slightly brown on top, about 20 minutes.
4. Remove and cool for 10 minutes on the cookie sheet. Cut the loaves into 1/2 inch-wide slices and lay them, cut side down on the cookie sheet. Bake for 10 minutes. Turn and bake for 10 minutes more. Remove the biscotti and cool on wire racks. Store in a container with a loose-fitting lid.

Spiced plum gingerbread cake.

Spiced Plum Gingerbread Cake

Makes one 10-inch bundt cake, or two 6-inch bundt cakes or one 15 x 10-inch sheet cake

Gingerbread is a traditional holiday favorite. Our friends Robert and Nancy Timans, the talented duo behind Thyme-Enz Harvest in Salisbury, Connecticut, use Harney's Spiced Plum ^H_T tea to impart flavor to the cake batter as well as for decoration and the pale pink coloring of the final glaze. It's a winner for sweets lovers of all ages.

¼ cup Spiced Plum^H_T tea leaves
8 tablespoons (1 stick) unsalted butter
½ cup (firmly packed) dark brown sugar
½ cup dark molasses
½ cup corn syrup
2¼ cups all-purpose flour
1½ teaspoons ground ginger
1½ teaspoons ground cinnamon

½ teaspoon ground cloves
½ teaspoon ground nutmeg
¼ teaspoon salt
2 eggs
Grated zest of 1 lemon
1 tablespoon lemon juice
2 teaspoons baking soda
4 cups confectioners' sugar

1. Preheat the oven to 350° F. Grease one 10-inch bundt pan, two 6-inch bundt pans or a 15 X 10-inch sheet pan.
2. Bring 1½ cups of water to a boil, add the tea, and steep for 5 minutes. Strain, pressing to extract as much liquid as possible. Don't worry if some of the leaves fall through.
3. Melt the butter, then stir it together with the brown sugar, molasses, and corn syrup. Set aside to cool.
4. Combine the flour, ginger, cinnamon, cloves, nutmeg, and salt in the bowl of a food processor and blend. Scrape in the butter-sugar mixture and blend. Add the eggs and lemon zest and blend until smooth.
5. Stir the baking soda into 1 cup of the tea. It will bubble up. Stir the mixture into the batter, mixing well, then scrape into the prepared pan(s). Bake for 40 to 45 minutes for a 10-inch bundt pan, 20 to 30 minutes for 6-inch bundt pans, or 40 to 45 minutes for a sheet pan. The top should be springy and a knife inserted near the center should come out clean. Remove pan and cool on a cake rack.
6. Combine the remaining tea with the lemon juice. Sift in the confectioners' sugar, whisking until a thick but spreadable icing is achieved. Pour over the cooled gingerbread cake and let set.

Green fruits in jasmine tea syrup.

Green Fruits in Jasmine Tea Syrup

Serves 6

Jasmine tea and sweetened lime juice transform a simple trio of green fruits into an ambrosial offering. Its memory will linger on your taste buds. Savor the fruit alone or with a scoop of green tea ice cream. This salad was created by Jane Pettigrew of London. The author of several highly regarded books about tea, Jane was the proprietor of the Tea Time tea shop in south London and, for many years, a consultant to the UK Tea Club.

> **2 teaspoons jasmine tea leaves**
> **½ cup sugar**
> **Grated zest of 1 lime**
> **Juice of 1 lime**
> **3 kiwi, peeled and sliced**
> **1 ripe honeydew melon, about 5 pounds, flesh scooped into little balls or diced**
> **8 ounces seedless green grapes, stemmed, washed, and cut in half**
> **Sprigs of fresh mint, for garnish**

1. Bring 1/3 cup of water just to a boil in a small saucepan. Add the jasmine tea, remove the pan from the heat, and infuse for 4 to 5 minutes. Strain into a clean pan, pressing to extract as much liquid as possible, and discard the tea leaves.
2. Add the sugar and lime zest to the pan. Over medium heat, stir until the sugar dissolves, then bring the liquid to a boil. Reduce the heat and simmer the syrup for 1 to 2 minutes. Remove the pan from the heat and stir in the lime juice.
3. Place the kiwi, melon, and grapes in a serving bowl and pour on the syrup. Cover and marinate in the refrigerator for 4 to 6 hours. Remove from the refrigerator at least 20 minutes before serving, toss gently, and garnish with mint.

Variations

Yellow Fruit Salad: Combine 4 apricots, 4 nectarines, 1 mango, 1 papaya, and 1 small pineapple all cut into cubes. Prepare a syrup flavored with Earl Grey tea and lemon juice instead of jasmine tea and lime. Proceed as for a green fruit salad.

Broiled pineapple with spicy cinnamon crème Anglaise sauce.

Broiled Pineapple with Spicy Cinnamon Crème Anglaise Sauce

Serves 6

Fresh pineapple slices quickly broiled with a light scattering of brown sugar make a sweet but slightly acidic partner for the sauce. The incredible concert of flavors—spicy cinnamon tea played against Cointreau and rum—will tantalize your tongue.

Spicy Cinnamon Crème Anglaise Sauce

1 cup heavy cream
2 teaspoons Hot Cinnamon Spice[HT] or other cinnamon spice–scented tea leaves
4 egg yolks
⅓ cup granulated sugar
¼ cup Cointreau or other orange-based liqueur
¼ cup light rum

6 slices fresh pineapple, about ¾ inch thick
3 tablespoons dark brown sugar
¼ cup chopped pecans

1. Combine the cream and tea in a small saucepan. Bring to a simmer then set aside to steep for 5 minutes. Strain through a fine strainer, pressing to extract as much liquid as possible. Meanwhile, combine the egg yolks and sugar in the top of a double boiler and beat with a wooden spoon until pale yellow, 1 to 2 minutes. Stir in the Cointreau, rum and infused cream. Bring water in the bottom of the double boiler to a boil, adjust the heat so the water just simmers, and insert the top into the bottom. Stir the mixture constantly until it thickly coats the back of the spoon, about 8 minutes.
2. Remove the top part from the heat and continue stirring the sauce for about 2 minutes more to cool slightly. Strain again, if desired, into a bowl, cover, and refrigerate the sauce until cool.
3. Adjust the broiler rack to about 4 inches from heat. Turn on the broiler.
4. Lay the pineapple slices on a cookie sheet or jelly-roll pan. Sprinkle with the brown sugar and broil until the sugar is bubbling and the pineapple is warmed through, about 3 minutes.
5. Ladle a generous pool of crème Anglaise onto 6 dessert plates or drizzle over the pineapple. Add a slice of pineapple, sprinkle with pecans, and serve.

Baked Peaches with Ricotta and Raspberry Tea Streusel

Serves 4

This delicious dessert of peach halves tucked under a layer of candied ginger---scented ricotta plus a streusel crust made with raspberry herbal tea takes minutes to make. We tried the same dessert with Vanilla tea[HT] and it was also a winner. Use the best quality canned peaches you can buy.

> 1 teaspoon unsalted butter, melted, to grease ramekins
> 4 canned peach halves packed in juice, drained
> ½ cup ricotta cheese, preferably whole milk
> 1 egg yolk
> 1½ teaspoons minced candied ginger
> ¼ cup blanched hazelnuts
> 2 tablespoons all-purpose flour
> 2 tablespoons sugar
> 1 teaspoon Raspberry Herbal[HT] tea leaves, finely ground
> Pinch of salt
> 2 tablespoons unsalted butter, cold, cut into small pieces

1. Preheat the oven to 375° F. Brush four 3 to 3 ½-inch ramekins with the butter and place a peach half, flat side up, in each.
2. Blend the ricotta, egg yolk, and candied ginger together in a bowl and spoon it over the peaches, covering them entirely.
3. Combine the hazelnuts, flour, sugar, tea leaves, and salt together in a food processor and process until the nuts are finely ground and blended. Add the butter and pulse just until the butter is the size of small peas. Spoon the streusel over the ricotta, shaking each ramekin to distribute the topping evenly.
4. Place the ramekins on a flat tray or cookie sheet and bake until the streusel topping is set and lightly browned, and the peach juices start bubbling up the sides of the ramekins, about 35 minutes. Remove, let cool for at least 15 minutes, and serve or refrigerate until chilled.

Two Queens Rice Pudding

Serves 6

Rice pudding is almost everyone's idea of comfort food. When made with two queens—basmati rice, whose name means "queen of fragrance" in Sanskrit, and Darjeeling tea, called "the queen of teas"—the results are a royal treat. Crown each serving with apricot preserves and the Spicy Cinnamon Crème Anglaise on page 93. ✿ Slowly infusing tea, then discarding the leaves, keeps the liquid from becoming bitter as it cooks.

2 cups whole milk
1½ tablespoons Darjeeling tea leaves
1 teaspoon unsalted butter
¾ cup water
½ cup basmati rice, rinsed 3 or 4 times in cold water
½ teaspoon salt
2 eggs, beaten
⅓ cup granulated sugar
1 teaspoon vanilla extract
¼ cup golden raisins, plumped in hot water and drained
Grated nutmeg, ground cinnamon, and finely ground Darjeeling tea leaves
    mixed with confectioners' sugar, for garnish
Apricot preserves (optional)
Spicy Cinnamon Crème Anglaise Sauce (page 93), optional

1. Heat the milk until bubbles form around the edge of the pan, remove from the heat, stir in the tea, and infuse for about 1 hour. Strain.
2. Preheat the oven to 350° F. Butter a 6-cup baking dish.
3. Combine the water and rice in a small saucepan, bring to a boil, then reduce the heat to a simmer, cover the pan, and cook until the water is absorbed, about 10 minutes. Leave covered for 5 minutes, then fluff the grains to separate. Stir the infused milk and salt into the rice and cook until the mixture begins to thicken, about 6 minutes.
4. Whisk the eggs, sugar, and vanilla together in a bowl. Slowly stir in the rice mixture, add the raisins, and blend. Scrape into the prepared dish, place in a larger pan, and transfer to the middle of the oven. Fill the larger pan with hot water to halfway up the side of the dish.

5. Bake until the pudding is firm and a knife inserted near the center comes out clean. Remove and let the pudding stand for at least 15 minutes. Sprinkle spiced confectioners' sugar over the top. To serve, ladle a generous pool of Crème Anglaise on each plate, spoon the rice pudding onto the plates, and top with a dollop of apricot preserves, and serve. Or refrigerate and serve cool.

Earl Grey Chocolate Mousse

Serves 6

The success of this soft mousse depends on pairing the finest dark chocolate available with high quality, aromatic bergamot-scented tea. It's simple to make yet quite sophisticated. The final dusting of ground tea and sugar, along with shaved chocolate, creates a decorative topping that echoes the mousse's flavors.

> 2 tablespoons water
> 1 tablespoon Earl Grey tea leaves
> 3½ ounces semisweet dark chocolate, chopped into small pieces
> 2 tablespoons unsalted butter
> Pinch of salt
> 3 eggs, separated
> 1 teaspoon vanilla extract
> ½ cup heavy cream
> ⅓ cup superfine sugar
> ½ teaspoon Earl Grey tea leaves
> 1 teaspoon superfine sugar
> Chocolate shavings, for garnish

1. Bring the water just to a boil, pour it over the tablespoon of tea, infuse for 5 minutes. Strain, pressing to extract as much liquid as possible, and set aside.
2. Combine the chocolate and butter in the top of a double boiler. Bring the water to a simmer and melt the chocolate. When it has just melted, remove the top from heat, add the salt, then whisk in the egg yolks, one at a time. Stir in 1 tablespoon of the infused tea and the vanilla.
3. Beat the egg whites into soft peaks. Stir a couple of spoonfuls of the whites into the chocolate mixture, then scrape the chocolate back into the bowl with the whites. Gently fold the remaining whites into the chocolate.
4. Whip the heavy cream and sugar into soft peaks, then fold it into mousse mixture. Transfer to a serving bowl, cover, and refrigerate until set. Before serving, combine the remaining tea and sugar in a spice/coffee grinder and pulverize. Sift the tea-sugar over the top of the mousse. Add chocolate shavings to the mousse, if desired.

Note about raw eggs: If you are concerned about using raw eggs, pasteurized liquid eggs are available in many supermarkets. When using raw eggs, it is wise to choose the freshest eggs available and to store them at 40° F or lower.

Jasmine–Tropical Fruit–Coconut Sorbet

Makes 1 quart

Taste the tropics in an exotic floral-scented sorbet that mixes jasmine-infused peach nectar, coconut milk, and banana. It's delicious alone or over fruit salad or pineapple slices. Adding an egg white gives a smoother texture to the mixture. They are now available pasteurized in local markets if you're concerned about using uncooked eggs (see page 97).

1½ cups peach nectar
1½ teaspoons jasmine tea leaves
1½ cups canned coconut milk
1 cup simple syrup (see Note)
1 large, ripe banana, mashed until smooth
1 egg white (optional)
Toasted coconut, for garnish (optional)

1. Bring the peach nectar just to a boil in a small saucepan. Stir in the jasmine tea, and infuse for 5 minutes. Strain. Blend the nectar, coconut milk, simple syrup, and banana together until smooth, then scrape into a metal or glass dish. Cover and freeze until solid, 8 hours or overnight.
2. Remove from freezer, cut into chunks, add the egg white, if using, and pulse in a food processor until smooth. Return to the freezer until frozen. Serve in small scoops with a few toasted coconut strands on top on each ball, if desired.

Note: For simple syrup, bring equal amounts of sugar and water slowly to a boil. Reduce the heat and let the sugar dissolve, stirring occasionally. Store in a clean glass container in the refrigerator.

Buttermilk–Vanilla Tea Sherbet

Makes 1 quart

Sherbet, unlike sorbet, is a frozen dessert with some milk in it. In this creamy confection, buttermilk is combined with aromatic vanilla tea, and the results are pleasing and light. Serve the sherbert with a fresh fruit salad.

1 cup superfine sugar
⅓ cup Vanilla^H_T tea leaves
3 cups buttermilk

1. Combine 1 cup of water and sugar in a small saucepan and bring to a boil. Stir to dissolve the sugar, pour the liquid over the tea leaves, steep for 5 minutes. Strain, pressing to extract as much liquid as possible.
2. Combine mixture with the buttermilk in the canister of an ice cream maker and freeze according to the manufacturer's directions.

Raspberry–Chocolate Mint Tea Frozen Yogurt

Makes 1 quart

Chocolate Mint tea is so delicious, some people say that drinking it is like drinking candy. If you combine a strong brew of the tea with puréed raspberries and yogurt, the hint of mint and chocolate played against the tangy berries is truly something to write home about!

½ **cup water**
⅓ **cup Chocolate Mint**^H_T **tea leaves**
1 **cup frozen raspberries, defrosted**
1 **cup sugar**
1 **quart plain yogurt**

1. Bring the water just to a boil, pour it over the tea leaves, steep for 5 minutes, then strain, pressing to extract as much liquid as possible. Set aside.
2. Combine the raspberries and sugar in a food processor and purée until smooth. Strain to remove the seeds, if desired. Stir the raspberries, tea, and yogurt together then pour into the canister of an ice cream maker and process according to the manufacturer's directions.

Chaice Cream with Blackberry Coulis

Makes 1 quart

Of all the sweet dishes made with tea, this is far and away my favorite. The subtle blend of Indian spiced tea, or chai, with cream is topped with a garnet ribbon of berry coulis.

Chaice Cream
1 cup whole milk
1 cup superfine sugar
½ cup Indian Spice^H_T tea leaves or other chai tea blend
3 cups heavy cream

Blackberry Coulis
12 ounces frozen blackberries, slowly defrosted
¾ cup blackberry jelly or preserves
Lemon juice

1. To make the chaice cream, stir the milk and sugar together in a small pan Heat until small bubbles form at the edge of the pan, stir in the tea leaves, and steep for 5 minutes. Strain, pressing to extract as much liquid as possible. Combine the infused milk and the cream in the canister of an ice cream maker and freeze according to the manufacturer's directions.
2. To make the coulis, purée the berries and jelly in a food processor until smooth. Strain through a fine sieve into a bowl. Stir in lemon juice to taste. Refrigerate until needed.

Great love affairs start with Champagne and end with tisane.

Honoré de Balzac

Beverages

Raspberry Teazer
Raspberry Champagne Cordial
Iced Cranberry-Apricot Tea
Orange-Scented Iced Mint Tea
Banana—Green Tea Smoothie
Mango Chai Lassi
Ginger Beer Float with Green Tea—Wasabi Ice Cream

Raspberry champagne cordial.

Raspberry Champagne Cordial

Makes 4 servings

A light champagne cocktail.

> **8 tablespoons Raspberry Herbal^H_T tea**
> **1 bottle (750 ml) champagne or prosecco, chilled**
> **8 to 12 fresh raspberries**

1. Bring ½ cup of water just to a boil, stir in the raspberry tea and sugar, and steep for 3 to 4 minutes. Strain and refrigerate.
2. When cool, pour 2 tablespoons chilled tea into each champagne flute. Add 5 to 6 ounces champagne and 2 to 3 raspberries to each, and serve.

Raspberry Teazer

Serves 2

A refreshing blend of raspberry herbal tea and seltzer. Use the same idea with other herbals, as well.

> 2 teaspoons Raspberry Herbal^HT tea leaves or other fruit tea
> 1 tablespoon sugar
> 8 ounces seltzer or sparkling water
> 2 thin slices lemon

1. Bring $1/2$ cup of water just to a boil, stir in the raspberry tea and sugar, and steep for 3 to 4 minutes. Strain and refrigerate.
2. When cool, divide the tea between 2 tall glasses, add ice, and pour in 4 ounces of seltzer or sparkling water. Add a lemon slice to each glass and serve.

Iced Cranberry-Apricot Punch

Makes 12 cups

For a refreshing iced drink, try this beautiful rose-colored chilled cranberry punch. Apricot nectar adds just the right amount of sweetness. To keep the flavors intense, the ice cubes are made with apricot nectar, as well. For an extra wallop, add a little peach schnapps.

5½ cups apricot nectar

8 cups brewed Cranberry Autumn Blend^HT or other fruit tea
   (about 4 tablespoons of loose tea leaves, 12 tea bags), chilled

¾ cup peach schnapps (optional)

1. Pour 1½ cup of the apricot nectar into 1 ice-cube tray. Freeze until solid. Refrigerate the remaining 4 cups apricot nectar until chilled.

2. Combine the cranberry tea and the chilled nectar in a large punch bowl. Stir in the schnapps, if using, add the nectar ice cubes, and serve.

Orange-Scented Iced Mint Tea

Makes 2 tall glasses of tea

A most refreshing drink for a hot afternoon or evening. It may be made with either mint tea or black tea infused with fresh mint leaves. A little orange juice and simple syrup are the sweeteners. ✿ Because iced tea becomes watery as the ice melts, brew a strong tea to start. Or use brewed tea for the ice cubes.

> **3 black tea bags of choice or mint tea bags**
> **4 mint leaves, coarsely chopped**
> **½ cup fresh orange juice**
> **2 tablespoons simple syrup (see page 98)**
> **Ice cubes**
> **Mint leaves for garnish**

1. Bring 2 cups of water just to a boil. Add the tea bags and chopped mint leaves and infuse for 5 minutes. Squeeze and remove the bags. Allow the tea to cool to lukewarm, then strain into 2 tall glasses.
2. Stir 1/4 cup of the orange juice and 1 tablespoon simple syrup into each glass. Add ice cubes, garnish with mint leaves, and serve.

Banana—Green Tea Smoothie

Serves 2

A quick and healthful breakfast shake.

1 cup low-fat or non-fat vanilla yogurt
1 ripe banana
2 tablespoons orange juice
2 teaspoons green tea leaves, finely ground
6 to 8 ice cubes

Combine the yogurt, banana, orange juice, and tea in an electric blender and purée until smooth. Add ice cubes and process just until thick and frothy. Pour into 2 tall glasses and serve.

Mango Chai Lassi

Serves 2

In India, lassi is a cool, refreshing drink made with yogurt and ice. Chai by this time is fairly well known as an Indian tea drink made with sweetened black tea leaves spiced with cardamom and cinnamon and boiled in milk. By combining the yogurt with Indian spiced tea and a puréed mango, you have a truly satisfying drink for hot summer days.

¼ cup light cream
1 tablespoon Indian Spice^H_T or other chai blend of tea leaves
1 large ripe mango, peeled, pitted, and cut into pieces
1 cup vanilla yogurt, preferably not non-fat
6 to 8 ice cubes
Mint leaves, for garnish (optional)

Bring the cream just to a simmer. Stir in the tea and steep for 5 minutes. Strain into an electric blender, pressing down on the tea to extract as much liquid as possible. Add the mango and yogurt and purée until smooth. Add the ice cubes and process until thick and frothy. Pour into 2 tall glasses, add a mint leaf to garnish, if desired, and serve.

Ginger Beer Float with Green Tea–Wasabi Ice Cream

Serves 4

Sam Mason, the pastry chef at Atlas, a New York City restaurant, transports an old-fashioned root beer float into a contemporary taste experience. Instead of mild-flavored vanilla, green tea–wasabi ice cream has a complex flavor with a subtle bite that plays well against the ginger beer. Fresh stalks of lemon grass add a stylish garnish.

> 1 teaspoon wasabi powder
> 1 teaspoon matcha green tea powder
> ¾ cup whole milk
> ¾ cup heavy cream
> ⅓ cup granulated sugar
> 3 egg yolks, beaten
> 4 stalks fresh lemon grass
> 4 bottles Stewart's Ginger Beer, chilled, available at specialty food stores

1. Combine the wasabi and green tea in a heavy bottomed medium saucepan. Slowly whisk in the milk and heavy cream until smooth. Bring the mixture to a boil over medium-high heat. Remove the pan from the heat, stir in the sugar, then gradually whisk in the egg yolks. Return the pan to medium heat and cook until slightly thickened, stirring constantly. Do not allow it to boil.

2. Pour the mixture into the canister of an ice cream maker and process according to the manufacturer's directions.

3. Scoop 2 generous balls of ice cream into each of 4 tall glasses. Add a stalk of lemon grass into each glass. Pour the ginger beer over the ice cream, and serve.

John Harney's Suggested Tea and Food Pairings

The marriage of food and drink is not a new concept: People do it all the time with food and wine. John Harney insists that the correct pairing of tea with food can make an ordinary meal much more delectable, and by extension, the correct pairing of tea used in cooking can also have a positive effect. These varieties of foods are paired with the teas that enhance their flavors. Use his suggestions as a guide and experiment on your own to find the perfect pairing to fit your palate.

All Breakfast Foods—Any strong black tea such as Assam, Ceylon, Kenya, Darjeeling

Light Meals—Darjeeling, Earl Grey, Assam, oolong, citron green, Lung Ching, sencha

Cheese—Sencha, Lung Ching, Earl Grey, all fruit-flavored teas

Asian and Indian Foods—Jasmine, oolong, Assam, Darjeeling, Lapsang souchong

Fish— Earl Grey, Darjeeling, sencha, Lung Ching

Beef, Lamb, and Pork—Jasmine, oolongs, Earl Grey, Keemun, Lapsang souchong

Chicken, Duck, and Goose—Oolong, Jasmine, Darjeeling, Assam

Afternoon Tea/High Tea—All teas

Dessert—Jasmine, French *vervaine*, French *tilleul*, Lung Ching, green flower green tea

Sleepy Time—Herbal or fruit-infusion teas such as chamomile, lemon, raspberry herbal

Acknowledgments

Joanna Pruess and John Harney wish to thank

Elyse Harney Morris—the most persistant and dedicated member of the Harney clan without whom this project would never have been completed.

Shawn Devaney—chef-owner of Sumptuous Foods, Boston, Massachusetts, for testing recipes and offering useful recommendations.

Pam Dove—for her astute suggestions while proofreading the manuscript.

Tom Eckerle—an exceptionally talented food photographer, through whose lens our tea dishes became real temptations.

Ceci Gallini—with her unerring eye for great style and props, she created perfect settings for our food photographs.

Dr. Mitchell Gaynor—medical director of the Weill Medical College in New York City, for writing the foreword to this book.

Becky Koh—our editor at The Lyons Press, who has been an enthusiastic champion of EAT TEA, and who made creating this book a fulfilling and pleasurable experience.

Danny Lee—former chef with John Harney at the White Hart Inn, Salisbury, Connecticut, and currently associate professor of Culinary Arts, the Culinary Institute of America, who taught us all to tea smoke great food, shared recipes, and generously prepared the tea-smoked duck for our photograph.

Dr. Erica Loutsch—an enthusiastic sampler of numerous tea dishes.

Kai Birger Nielson—for contributing to the tea timeline.

James Norwood Pratt—tea scholar and author, for sharing his abundant knowledge on the subject with us.

Brad Troxell—chef in Farmington, Connecticut, with twenty years of food-service experience, and a longtime friend of the Harney family, for testing recipes and offering valuable suggestions.

Rick and Charlie Waln—Joanna's neighbors extraordinaire, for eagerly sampling more and different versions of so many dishes.

Melissa Vaughan—Tom Eckerle's culinary intern, whose skills, tireless energy, and good humor were so valuable in making the photo sessions a success.

Index